Hands-on Test-Driven Development

Greg Donald

Hands-on Test-Driven Development

Using Ruby, Ruby on Rails, and RSpec

Apress®

Greg Donald
Clarksville, TN, USA

ISBN-13 (pbk): 978-1-4842-9747-6   ISBN-13 (electronic): 978-1-4842-9748-3
https://doi.org/10.1007/978-1-4842-9748-3

Managing Director, Apress Media LLC: Welmoed Spahr
Acquisitions Editor: Melissa Duffy
Development Editor: James Markham
Coordinating Editor: Gryffin Winkler

Cover designed by eStudioCalamar

Cover image by Pexels@Pixabay.com

Distributed to the book trade worldwide by Apress Media, LLC, 1 New York Plaza, New York, NY 10004, U.S.A. Phone 1-800-SPRINGER, fax (201) 348-4505, e-mail orders-ny@springer-sbm.com, or visit www.springeronline.com. Apress Media, LLC is a California LLC and the sole member (owner) is Springer Science + Business Media Finance Inc (SSBM Finance Inc). SSBM Finance Inc is a **Delaware** corporation.

For information on translations, please e-mail booktranslations@springernature.com; for reprint, paperback, or audio rights, please e-mail bookpermissions@springernature.com.

Apress titles may be purchased in bulk for academic, corporate, or promotional use. eBook versions and licenses are also available for most titles. For more information, reference our Print and eBook Bulk Sales web page at http://www.apress.com/bulk-sales.

Any source code or other supplementary material referenced by the author in this book is available to readers on GitHub (https://github.com/Apress). For more detailed information, please visit https://www.apress.com/gp/services/source-code.

Paper in this product is recyclable

This book is dedicated to my wife and best friend, Sunni. She has been a constant source of support and encouragement during the writing of this book.

Contents

About the Author

Greg Donald has been a professional software engineer since 1996 and has worked with Ruby on Rails since 2006. Prior to that, he worked on many Perl and PHP projects, finding the applications messy and hard to maintain. He became a test driven development enthusiasts after having seen the results of software written in various forms, and determining no style was more successful than TDD. He decided to write this book to promote TDD and share his positive experiences using it.

About the Technical Reviewer

Eldon is a senior technologist, creator, and United States Marine Corps veteran. He's the author of two software development books. His career has allowed him to work across a wide variety of technologies and domains. His career has taken him from working in successful startups in roles ranging from senior developer to chief architect to working as a principal technologist for a global software consulting firm, helping enterprises and companies rescue software projects and/or evolve their software delivery capabilities.

These days, he works as a technical fellow with a mission of raising the bar of software development globally for a technology company providing tools, AI, and research to advance the rule of law.

Currently, he lives in Florida where he enjoys scuba diving and creating video content.

Introduction

1

Hello, and welcome! I'm very excited to share with you my book about test-driven software development. I've been a software engineer for over 25 years, and I've seen the results of software written using many different styles and techniques. It wasn't so long ago that we didn't even write tests for our software. At some point, some very smart people realized that writing tests for our software was actually a good idea. Our tests would provide us with confidence that our software worked as expected and even more importantly keep us from getting phone calls in the middle of the night to fix things that would break in production.

Not long after we started writing tests, some other very smart people realized that writing our tests first would give us an opportunity to think about what we were going to write before we would write it. It would give us a target to aim at, in effect. This was the birth of test-driven development (TDD). TDD is a style of software development where we write our tests first, see that they are failing as expected, and only then do we pursue writing the code to make those tests pass.

This is the central idea of my book. We will think about what we want to do, then we will capture that idea with a properly failing test. We will then write the code to make the test pass. We will then refactor our code to make it better, or prettier, or less repetitive, and then we will write another test. We will repeat this process over and over until we have a fully functional web application.

Let's get started!

What Are We Building?

As you pick up this book and look inside at the first few pages, you may be wondering, what exactly are we going to build? I'm so glad you asked! We will build a **fully functional blog**! A "*blog*," short for "weblog" or "web log," is a web application that allows its administrator (you) to post articles to the Web. Instead of downloading premade blog software, for example, WordPress,[1] we're going to build our own blog software from scratch.

We'll be using the Ruby[2] programming language and the Ruby on Rails[3] web framework to build everything. These are the best tools for the job, in my opinion. Ruby is a very expressive and powerful programming language, and Ruby on Rails is a very powerful web framework.

---

[1] https://wordpress.org/

[2] https://ruby-lang.org/

[3] https://rubyonrails.org/

© The Author(s), under exclusive license to APress Media, LLC, part of Springer Nature 2024   1
G. Donald, *Hands-on Test-Driven Development*,
https://doi.org/10.1007/978-1-4842-9748-3_1

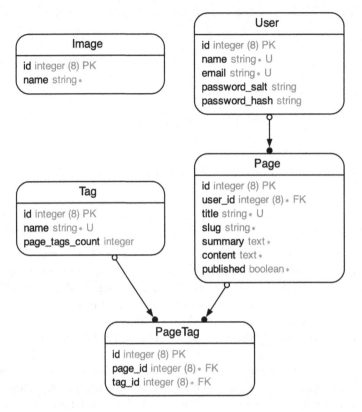

Figure 1-1 Blog database diagram

We'll use the **test-driven development (TDD)** style of software design and engineering, which means we'll write failing tests first and only then write our implementation code to get our failing tests passing.

We'll use the RSpec[4] testing framework to write our tests. RSpec describes itself as a tool for performing "**behavior-driven development**" and is in fact the best tool available for testing Ruby code. If you've never used RSpec before, don't worry; in this book, I'll cover more than enough to get you started and productive.

Our blog will be a simple web application overall, but will be complex enough to demonstrate the test-driven development style of software development. Our blog will allow us to create and update pages as well as search them by keyword and tag them for easy categorization.

Let's take a look at our database design next.

Our Database

We will use the PostgreSQL[5] relational database management system (RDBMS) to store our blog's data. When it comes to free and open source databases, PostgreSQL is best in its class.

At the end of the book, our database design will look similar to the diagram in Figure 1-1.

---

[4]https://rspec.info/

[5]https://postgresql.org/

We'll go into much more detail about our database design in later chapters, but I want to give you an initial idea of what we'll be building early on. We will have database tables for **users**, **pages**, **tags**, and **images**. Our image table is not connected to any of the other previously mentioned tables. Our tag table is connected to our page table through our **page_tags** join table. Each of our pages will belong to a single user. With this design, we can have more than one user, and each user can be an author of many pages.

We will build up our database design as we go, adding new tables and columns as we need them, as that's the nature of practicing proper test-driven development.

Why Another TDD Book?

The main goal of this book is to provide a practical, hands-on introduction to the test-driven style of software design and engineering.

Many books on the topic of test-driven development have been written before this one. Some of them are actually very good, but none of them were written in the practical, hands-on style of this book. In fact, very few books are written in this style.

This book covers the building of an entire web application, from start to finish. Our focus application, a blog, is the most practical thing I could think to build, given my audience of software engineering readers. Every software engineer has their own online blog, right? A blog is simple enough that it can be covered in a single book, but complex enough that it can be used to demonstrate my favorite parts of RSpec while building a Ruby on Rails web application.

Most other TDD books are written in a *small-problem* sort of writing style. They cover single topics, one at a time, barely more than a reference guide. They do not cover the entire process of building a software application from start to finish, using TDD. As a result, they are, in my opinion, less practical and much less useful for actually learning practical TDD.

My Motivation

About five years ago, I joined a team of software engineers who were busy working on a very important (people's lives were at stake) large-scale web application. They were several months into it at the time, and there were deadlines. The application was being written in Ruby on Rails, and the team was using TDD to build it. They were practicing *Extreme Programming* (XP),[6] as described by Kent Beck,[7] pretty much to the letter. I had heard of TDD and XP before, but had never actually practiced them. I had never even pair-programmed[8] an entire day prior to joining the team. I was eager to learn, and little did I know at the time that I was working with some of the best software engineers I had ever met.

These girls and guys were amazingly agile. They refactored their code constantly. They were always looking for ways to reduce code complexity and improve their processes. They were constantly learning new things, and they were always teaching each other new things. They were very passionate about their craft and passionate about leveling up their team even more so.

I soon realized I was in over my head. I was a *n00b* to the team, to TDD, and to XP. They did not seem to care about any of that.

---

[6]www.extremeprogramming.org/

[7]http://wiki.c2.com/?KentBeck

[8]http://wiki.c2.com/?PairProgramming

They were very patient with me, and they were completely willing to teach me everything they knew. They taught me how to practice proper TDD and XP. They taught me how to write failing tests first and how to write code that is easy to test. They taught me how to write tests that supplied courage for when I would later perform fearless refactoring.

Over the next couple of years, I became a much better software engineer. The first major change I noticed in myself was how I had stopped worrying about code I had recently pushed into production. I was no longer thinking about code breaking in production during my off hours or how these sorts of breakages were often followed by an emergency phone call to hurry to fix things. I had stopped worrying about code breaking because I knew my code was completely covered with well-written tests and very unlikely to break.

Another change I noticed in myself was that I was writing cleaner code. I was writing code that was easier to later understand. I was only writing the code that was necessary to get my tests into a passing state. I got into a pattern of knowing that once my tests pass, my implementation work was done. Moving on to refactor any ugliness or code duplication is my *only* next step before writing my *next* failing test.

I'm telling you all of this because I want you to understand how I've come to learn and respect test-driven development. I learned it by doing it, for many years, with a team of experts. I know that developing software using TDD produces better software than not using TDD to develop software. I know this because I have seen the final results with my own eyes.

Why You Should Trust Me

I've been a *computer programmer* for a long time. If we're counting uncompensated work, then I've been programming since 1984, when I wrote my first bits of BASIC[9] code on my grandpa's TI-99/4A,[10] saving my work to a cassette tape. I went on to write more advanced programs and games in BASIC at my junior high school, where we had Apple IIe[11] computers in our computer lab. A few years later, in high school, we had IBM PC clones[12] in our computer lab, and it was at this time I learned to program in Turbo Pascal.[13]

I joined the US Navy in 1990 and didn't have much contact with computers for the next few years. When I got out in 1995, I discovered the *World Wide Web* was a thing, and I became instantly hooked on my newly found favorite hobby, building web pages. I taught myself HTML and enough Perl[14] to be dangerous, and by late 1996, I had landed my first paid programming job as a *web developer* working on Perl-based shopping cart software.

So if we're counting compensated work, I've been a self-taught professional software engineer since late 1996. I've written code in almost every major programming language and on many different operating systems and platforms. My focus has been on web development for the most part, but I also have significant experience working on mobile applications and games, in native code, for both Android and iOS. I was an early publisher on Google's Android platform, having the first published Blackjack game there.

---

[9]http://hopl.info/showlanguage.prx?exp=176

[10]www.ti994.com/

[11]www.old-computers.com/museum/computer.asp?st=1&c=83

[12]www.ibm.com/ibm/history/exhibits/pc/pc_1.html

[13]http://progopedia.com/implementation/turbo-pascal/

[14]www.perl.org/

In 2005–2006, I started working with Ruby on Rails. I had some experience with Ruby before that, automating processes on Linux, but didn't get into Ruby seriously until I started working with Rails. Rails was my first experience using the *model-view-controller*[15] (MVC) design pattern, and it was a revelation to me. Prior to that, I had worked on many Perl and PHP[16] projects, and I had always thought they were messy and hard to maintain, and there was certainly never anything like a test-suite present.

I tell you all this to instill a bit of trust. I've seen software written many different ways, and I've seen the results of those pursuits. I've never seen software written using TDD that was not better than software written without TDD.

Audience and Prerequisites

I've seen many programmers, both beginners and those who have been programming for years, who can't begin to imagine writing failing tests first and only then writing the code to make those tests pass. This book will be useful in teaching you how to do that, providing confidence and courage.

This book is written for *beginner* to *intermediate* Ruby programmers who are interested in learning to use TDD with RSpec to test and build web applications using Ruby on Rails. It is assumed that you have some experience with Ruby and Ruby on Rails and that you have read the *Getting Started with Rails*[17] guide that's available for Rails, or something similar.

How to Read This Book

This book should be read in a linear fashion, from beginning to end. The chapters are numbered and should be read in that order. This is not a reference guide and does not provide complete coverage of any particular topic. Those kinds of reference books already exist for many of the topics discussed in this book, and duplicating their authors' efforts would not provide much value.

This is a *work-along* book. Every effort has been made to make this book self-contained, so that you can read it from cover to cover and not need to refer to any other resources. Nevertheless, I've been quite liberal in my use of footnote references to other resources, so please do visit them for additional information on unfamiliar topics.

---

[15]http://wiki.c2.com/?ModelViewControllerHistory

[16]www.php.net/

[17]https://guides.rubyonrails.org/getting_started.html

What Is Test-Driven Development?

2

Test-driven development is a powerful software development technique where the test (or *spec*) is written *before* the implementation code. Initially, the test will fail because the implementation code does not exist yet. This situation with a failing test is expected and is known to *drive out* minimal implementation code changes or additions to get the failing test into a passing state. It may sound complicated at first, but with a thorough demonstration of the benefits, followed by a bit of practice, you'll begin to prefer doing things this way.

But what happens when we don't do test-driven development? What happens when we write our tests *after* the implementation code? I'm so glad you asked!

Problems with Late Test Writing

In this section, we will explore some of the problems with writing tests after the implementation code has already been written.

No Code Design

When we write our tests *after* the implementation code, we're typically not thinking too much about the design of our code. We're mostly just writing tests to make sure our code works. This is a very different, and less thoughtful, mindset than when we're writing tests *before* the implementation code.

When we write our tests before the implementation code, we're thinking about the design of our code, how we want our code to behave and be used. We're hopefully also thinking about how we want our code to be extended in the future, probably by us.

Passing by Accident

When we write our tests *after* the implementation code, we will inevitably write tests that **pass by accident**. This is because we're not taking the time to see the tests fail first.

We should **never** trust tests that we did not see fail first.

© The Author(s), under exclusive license to APress Media, LLC, part of Springer Nature 2024
G. Donald, *Hands-on Test-Driven Development*,
https://doi.org/10.1007/978-1-4842-9748-3_2

The one exception is that you may work on a team where you will not actually see every single newly written test fail before it's made to pass. Obviously, we don't want to delete our team members' tests and hard work. But we should always have a high degree of skepticism about our own tests and pursue seeing them fail appropriately.

This advice of trusting tests based on individual experience with seeing them fail also comes with a bit of counter advice: don't ever be afraid to delete a test that cannot be made to fail by temporarily reversing or commenting implementation code. Delete unfailable tests as soon as possible. Your continuous integration[1] server will thank you.

Code Spikes

Sometimes, we may need to explore our ideas, with code, a bit before we know what our desired behavior will be. Often, we write this sort of code knowing up front we will eventually throw it away. This act of writing throwaway code is known as *code spiking* and almost certainly also accompanies the deliberate act of not writing any tests beforehand. This situation should be rare, and we should always be thinking about how we can write tests that *will* fail when we're done with exploring our ideas.

Practically speaking, anytime I'm done with spiking some bits of code, I will comment the code out and then proceed with writing failing tests. I then uncomment my spiked code, a bit at a time usually, to get my tests passing. This is a very useful technique for safely exploring ideas with code and for junior TDD practitioners who have a hard time with test writing.

We've now explored some of the problems with writing tests *after* the implementation code. Let's now explore the benefits of writing tests *before* the implementation code.

The Red-Green-Refactor Development Cycle

Test-driven development can be thought of as a three-phase development cycle as shown in Figure 2-1.

1. Red
2. Green
3. Refactor

Let's step through each phase and discuss it in more detail, with simple but practical code examples.

Red Phase

In the *red* phase of the TDD cycle, an initially failing test is written. Most often, this will just be a single test. It should be a minimal concept or idea designed to *drive out* a desired behavior.

---

[1]http://wiki.c2.com/?ContinuousIntegration

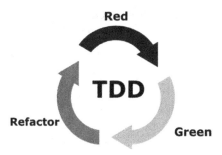

Figure 2-1 The red-green-refactor development cycle

Imagine we want a method that adds two numbers and returns a result. An example failing test might be

```
it 'equals 4' do
  result = add(2, 2)
  expect(result).to eq(4)
end
```

This test will fail because there is a call to an add method that currently does not exist. This is a very useful test because it will focus our attention on our implementation code changes.

Notice how most of the test is written in a way that it flows like a couple of English sentences. This is RSpec's developer-friendly DSL in action; our tests are easy to read and understand.

Green Phase

Next, we add our implementation code changes to turn the *red* failing test into a *green* passing test.

The first error we get is the missing method error. We could add an empty method to satisfy the error:

```
def add
end
```

After adding that, our test will still fail, but it will fail with a different error. It will complain about the argument signature being wrong. We can fix that error with adding the desired arguments to the method signature:

```
def add(x, y)
end
```

Finally, we get to the end where the empty method returns `nil` instead of the value of the arguments being added together. We can fix that by implementing the arguments being added together and returned:

```
def add(x, y)
  x + y
end
```

It depends on the situation and your own experience level with the codebase for how fine-grained you choose to have your red-green-refactor loop operate. I think stepping through it like this is a good way to get started with TDD, but I certainly don't always do it this way. I sometimes even find myself writing more than one test at a time and then implementing the code to make them all eventually pass.

Refactor Phase

After the green phase, we reach the refactor phase. In this simple example, there's not much that can be refactored, but that's a very short-term problem for anything larger than a small hello-world sort of program. Imagine if you decided to rename the `add` method's `x` and `y` arguments to something else; perhaps you decide `a` and `b` would be more appropriate. The updated `add` method might then look like this:

```
def add(a, b)
  a + b
end
```

This sort of refactoring is considered safe since there is a test that will inform us if we break the implementation code. When we run the test again, it should still pass, letting us know our refactor was successful.

Any sort of refactoring done outside of proper test coverage is dangerous. Software engineers who practice test-driven development always prefer implementation code changes be done *under test*, even if that means backfilling missing test coverage first.

This section gave you a small taste of what you're in store for with the rest of the book.

Wash, Rinse, and Repeat

The instructions from the back of the shampoo bottle "*wash, rinse, and repeat*" imply an endless cycle of performing the same tasks again and again (or just twice depending on how literal you take the meaning of the word "repeat"). In TDD, this is exactly what we do. At the end of our refactor phase, we're ready to repeat the cycle and begin with a new failing test. A repetitious *red, green, refactor* loop informs us sooner rather than later when we've accidentally gone down a wrong path.

Advantages of Building Software Using TDD

In the next section, we will discuss the benefits of practicing test-driven development. These benefits are not just for the individual software engineer but also for the entire software engineering team.

Code Design

Test-driven development encourages us to think through our code design *before* implementing the code.

Every experienced software engineer has at some point in their career worked on a poorly designed application codebase. Often, these codebases have little or no test coverage, making refactoring and improving them very dangerous. Even the smallest change *over here* could cause some unexpected breakage *over there*. Surprisingly, broken code in production is no fun at all!

TDD gives us the power to make small incremental changes to our code design without the danger of unknowingly breaking things. Sure, sometimes our changes do break things; that's to be expected. But with adequate test coverage, these breakages will alert us as soon as possible, so we can make informed decisions about the direction of our evolving code design. We may choose to stop and undo our latest change, or we may choose to push on and repair our test failures. Either way, it causes us to consider everything more carefully before we proceed.

No Broken Windows

Broken Window Theory refers to urban decay. A single unfixed broken window in a neighborhood leads to a second broken window and so on until the entire community is in complete disrepair. This way of thinking about urban decay easily lends itself to how we think about software engineering.

The idea of a broken window in software engineering can manifest itself in different ways.

The first way that comes to my mind is when a bug appears in the codebase and (hopefully) causes a test to begin to fail, and then for whatever reason no one immediately pursues fixing it. The longer the unfixed bug lives on, the more risk there is for data corruption, user dissatisfaction, lesser revenues, or security issues.

Another type of broken window is a sort of generic term we software engineers refer to as *technical debt*, the unpaid time we still owe to the codebase that we didn't pay when it was initially due. This can be anything like outdated software dependencies or duplicate lines of code that need to be factored out into a shared code module.

The longer these broken windows accumulate on top of each other, the more effort required to fix them when we do eventually get around to it.

"I'll fix it, no need to remind me every 8 months!"

The most important phase of TDD is the green phase. We never proceed with new development without getting our tests back to a fully passing state. A "green" codebase tells us all known software bugs are fixed and any recently updated software dependencies are working as expected.

Good software engineers fix their broken windows as soon as possible!

Maintaining Focus

TDD keeps you focused on the problem, and just the problem.

There's a software principle and acronym YAGNI[2] that means *you aren't gonna need it*. TDD-focused software engineers believe, when given a user story with well-written acceptance criteria, it is the job of the software engineers to do no more and no less than exactly what the story requests be done.

There is real danger in adding things not explicitly requested in the user story. Another engineer could already be adding the thing you are thinking to add while working on *their* current story. Or there could be a follow-on story where the new behavior is described there. We just don't know what tomorrow's user stories will bring, and with finite resources, it's better to not guess.

Acceptance Testing

TDD lends itself naturally to automatically validated code. If your tests closely match the given acceptance criteria, then your implementation code will usually result in the desirable feature changes and behavior.

A very nice side effect of using TDD is that it tells you exactly when you are done working on a user story. If all the new acceptance criteria tests are passing and there are no more refactorings in sight, then it's usually time to deliver the story. So ship it!

Code Quality

TDD helps software engineers maintain high code quality. Implementation code is typically leaner and more precise than code written outside of TDD. Code refactorings occur more often when tests exist, helping to reduce the danger of change. We software engineers feel more empowered to pursue code cleanups and refactorings when we know the risk of breaking anything is lower.

These ways of thinking about software engineering play out across software engineering teams too. An individual team member is much more likely to care about code quality if other engineers are seen caring too.

Summary

This chapter discussed the philosophy and benefits of practicing test-driven development. You may not yet be convinced that TDD is the right way to go; I certainly wasn't convinced early on. It just takes time to reprogram your brain to think to write the tests first, especially if you've been writing software for a while already. Don't give up; the struggle is worth the reward!

---

[2] www.techtarget.com/whatis/definition/You-arent-gonna-need-it

Getting Started with Ruby

In this chapter, we'll install tools we can use to manage our installed Ruby versions. We will issue commands to our local operating system via the command-line interface[1] (CLI) using a shell interpreter, which depending on your operating system is likely to be bash or zsh. On macOS, we can use the *Terminal* application to issue these commands, and similar programs are available on other operating systems:

1. Homebrew
2. rbenv
3. Ruby

Installing Homebrew

On macOS, I use Homebrew[2] to install most of my local software development stack. There's a shell command on the Homebrew homepage I use to install it:

```
URL=https://raw.githubusercontent.com/Homebrew/\
install/HEAD/install.sh
bash -c "$(curl -fsSL $URL)"
```

If trusting this way of installing Homebrew via direct URL execution makes you nervous, you can install Homebrew manually too:

https://docs.brew.sh/Installation

---

[1] www.codecademy.com/article/command-line-interface

[2] https://brew.sh

© The Author(s), under exclusive license to APress Media, LLC, part of Springer Nature 2024
G. Donald, *Hands-on Test-Driven Development*,
https://doi.org/10.1007/978-1-4842-9748-3_3

Homebrew also works on Linux and Windows Subsystem for Linux. If you're working under those environments, you can find more information here:

https://docs.brew.sh/Homebrew-on-Linux

Installing rbenv

As previously mentioned, we will use `rbenv`[3] to manage our Ruby installations. Using `rbenv` allows us to easily switch between different versions of Ruby with just a few keystrokes. This provides us with flexibility to use different versions of Ruby for different projects and to easily upgrade to newer versions of Ruby when they are released.

We can install `rbenv` with the following `brew` command:

```
brew install rbenv
```

After installation, `rbenv` then requires initialization in our command SHELL.[4] We will place this initialization in our `.bashrc` or `.zshrc` file depending on which SHELL we are using. This will allow us to use `rbenv` commands in our shell and have it automatically configured anytime we start a new shell.

`zsh` users will add this to the end of ".zshrc" and then source it:

```
echo 'eval "$(rbenv init - zsh)"' >> ~/.zshrc

. ~/.zshrc
```

`bash` users will perform a similar command and then source it:

```
echo 'eval "$(rbenv init - bash)"' >> ~/.bashrc

. ~/.bashrc
```

If you're not sure which SHELL you're using, you can find out by issuing the command `echo $SHELL`.

Installing Ruby

Installing Ruby will require we first install some dependencies. Our Ruby compilation will fail or may not function correctly if we are missing these dependencies. We can install them from Homebrew using the `brew` command again:

---

[3] https://github.com/rbenv/rbenv
[4] https://datacarpentry.org/shell-genomics/01-introduction/

```
brew install openssl readline
```

Now that we have our dependencies installed, we can use "rbenv" to install the latest version of Ruby:

```
rbenv install 3.2.2
```

This command may take several minutes or longer to complete depending on our system specs.

Please note, the latest version will probably be different by the time you're reading this book. You can find the current latest version by running the rbenv list command with grep and sort, like this:

```
rbenv install -L | grep -E '^\d' | sort -V
```

Using grep with the proper regular expression removes all the more exotic implementations of Ruby from the list: jruby, rbx, and others. In this book, we're going to use the original MRI[5] (Matz's Ruby Interpreter) version of Ruby, created by Yukihiro Matsumoto[6] and friends.

After rbenv installs your chosen version of Ruby, you can set that version to be your global version:

```
rbenv global 3.2.2
```

Now we can run the which command and see that ruby and the Ruby gem command are both installed via rbenv shims:

```
which ruby
/Users/gd/.rbenv/shims/ruby

which gem
/Users/gd/.rbenv/shims/gem
```

If these which commands do not work for you right away, you may need to restart your terminal or shell application.

rbenv shims are used to provide us the ability to easily switch between Ruby versions. If you would like to pursue a deeper understanding of rbenv shims, more information is available.[7]

---

[5]www.ruby-lang.org

[6]https://dbpedia.org/page/Yukihiro_Matsumoto

[7]https://github.com/rbenv/rbenv#understanding-shims

Let's now check that `ruby` is actually executable and is the version we installed:

```
ruby -v
ruby 3.2.2 (2023-03-30 revision e51014f9c0)
```

Success!

It's also worth mentioning that there are other ways to accomplish what we've done here. For example, instead of using `rbenv` we could have instead used `rvm`.[8] On macOS, instead of Homebrew we could have used MacPorts.[9] My point is that if you already have a preference for other tooling to manage your Ruby installations, then feel free to use them.

Summary

In this chapter, we installed Homebrew, `rbenv`, and Ruby. We learned to use the `brew` command to install software on our local machine. We also learned how to use `rbenv` to manage our Ruby versions. In the future, we can easily switch to a new version of Ruby with a single command. We can also now have any number of Ruby projects using different versions of Ruby.

---

[8] https://rvm.io/
[9] www.macports.org/

Getting Started with Ruby on Rails

4

In the previous chapter, we installed the Ruby language itself. In this chapter, we will install the Ruby on Rails[1] framework and some additional tools Ruby software engineers use for Ruby on Rails application development:

1. Bundler
2. Ruby on Rails
3. PostgreSQL

Installing Bundler

Bundler[2] is a package manager that manages the dependencies of a Ruby application. Our project will use Bundler to manage the dependencies of our Ruby on Rails application specifically. Bundler is a Ruby gem, so we will use the Ruby gem[3] command to install it:

```
gem install bundler
```

This should produce output similar to the following:

```
Successfully installed bundler-2.4.10
Parsing documentation for bundler-2.4.10
Done installing documentation for bundler after 0 seconds
1 gem installed
```

By the time you read this, the latest version of Bundler may be different, so feel free to use the latest version of Bundler available.

---

[1]https://rubyonrails.org/

[2]https://bundler.io/

[3]https://guides.rubygems.org/rubygems-basics/

© The Author(s), under exclusive license to APress Media, LLC, part of Springer Nature 2024
G. Donald, *Hands-on Test-Driven Development*,
https://doi.org/10.1007/978-1-4842-9748-3_4

Installing Ruby on Rails

Ruby on Rails is a web application framework written in the Ruby programming language. It's designed to make programming web applications faster and easier by making opinionated decisions about what every web developer needs in their web development software stack. Ruby on Rails enables us to write less code while accomplishing more than any other language and framework, given similar effort.

As a framework, Ruby on Rails consists of several individual Ruby gems, but we only need to install a single gem to pull everything in at once. Let's use the Ruby gem command to install the "**rails**" gem:

```
gem install rails
```

This command will generate a lot of output and should include something similar to the following:

```
Successfully installed rails-7.0.4.3
Parsing documentation for rails-7.0.4.3
Done installing documentation for rails after 0 seconds
1 gem installed
```

By the time you read this, the latest version of Rails may be different, so feel free to use the latest available version.

Installing PostgreSQL

PostgreSQL[4] is a very popular relational database management system (RDBMS) used by a lot of Ruby on Rails applications and other web applications in general. We will use PostgreSQL to store the data for our Ruby on Rails application.

As you may have guessed, PostgreSQL is available to install from Homebrew, so we will use the brew command to install it:

```
brew install postgresql@14
```

Again, by the time you read this, the latest version of PostgreSQL may be different, so feel free to use the latest version of PostgreSQL available. The PostgreSQL developers put a lot of effort into maintaining backwards compatibility, so there's usually no need to worry about using the latest version of PostgreSQL.

---

[4]www.postgresql.org/

After installing PostgreSQL, we need to start the PostgreSQL server:

```
brew services start postgresql@14
```

As a sanity check, we should use the PostgreSQL `psql` command to connect to the PostgreSQL server and run a simple SQL query:

```
psql -d postgres -c "SELECT version()"
```

This should yield a result containing the version of PostgreSQL we just installed. If it does not work, and you get an error message about `psql` not being found, you may need to add the directory where the `psql` program was installed to your `PATH` environment variable. You can do this by adding the following line to your ~/.zshrc (or ~/.bashrc) file:

```
export PATH="/opt/homebrew/bin:$PATH"
```

This will prepend the directory path /opt/homebrew/bin to your existing $PATH and then re-export the new value to your shell environment. After making the change, run the following command to source and re-apply the contents of your ~/.zshrc file:

```
. ~/.zshrc
```

If /opt/homebrew/bin is not the location where `psql` was installed, you will need to change the path to the location where `psql` was actually installed. It may, for example, be installed in /usr/local/bin or some other location like /opt/homebrew/Cellar/postgresql/14.x/bin.

Installing Node.js

Node.js[5] is a JavaScript runtime environment that we need for our Ruby on Rails application development. We won't be using Node directly, but Rails commands, like the `rails new` command, will use Node.js to compile JavaScript assets for our application as we develop.

Node.js is available to install from Homebrew, so we will use the `brew` command to install it:

```
brew install node
```

---

[5] https://nodejs.org/

After the install completes, we can see that Node.js is installed by running the following commands:

```
which node
node --version
npm --version
npx --version
```

If these commands do not complete with successful output, you may need to add the directory where the node, npm, and npx programs were installed to your PATH environment variable, as we did with the psql program earlier.

Now that we have Node.js installed, we can use it to install some Javascript packages Rails will need for our Ruby on Rails application development and very importantly when we run the rails new command shortly. We will use the npm command to install the esbuild, nodemon, and sass packages:

```
npm install -g esbuild nodemon sass
```

Now we are ready to create our new Ruby on Rails application.

Creating a New Ruby on Rails Application

In this book, we will create a Ruby on Rails application in the form of a blog. We will use the Ruby on Rails rails new[6] command to create our new Ruby on Rails application. Before proceeding, let's discuss our rails new command-line options we will use to configure our new Ruby on Rails application creation.

We are going to use RSpec for testing, so for now we will use the -skip-test option to tell Ruby on Rails to skip creating its own test directory and related files. There's currently no command-line option to add RSpec (which is preposterous), so we will add RSpec manually later.

We will use the --database=postgresql option to tell Ruby on Rails to configure our app for use with PostgreSQL as the database for our application. This option will cause a Gemfile entry to be added for the pg gem and will preconfigure our config/database.yml file for use with PostgreSQL.

JavaScript support has evolved a lot in recent years, and Ruby on Rails has a new way of handling JavaScript dependencies called importmap.[7] We will use that along with esbuild[8] for our JavaScript bundler.

Finally, we will use Bootstrap[9] for our CSS framework. Bootstrap is a very popular CSS framework that provides lots of convenient CSS classes to make building web applications easier for both web and mobile apps.

---

[6]https://guides.rubyonrails.org/command_line.html#rails-new

[7]https://github.com/rails/importmap-rails

[8]https://esbuild.github.io/

[9]https://getbootstrap.com

Before you blast me with an email about how Bootstrap is the old way and how Tailwind is the new hotness, I know. I'm going to use Bootstrap for this book because it's what I know best and it's what I like.

Another consideration is in what directory do we run the `rails new` command? The simple answer is that it doesn't matter much. The `rails new` command we're going to use makes a directory and puts everything inside it. You can then move this directory around to where you want it to live, now or in the future.

I personally like to store my Rails-specific code in my ~/workspace/rails directory, so I will run the `rails new` command after I change into that directory, like this:

```
cd ~/workspace/rails
```

Be sure to use whatever directory you prefer for your Rails code.

```
rails new \
    --skip-test \
    --database=postgresql \
    --javascript=esbuild \
    --css=bootstrap \
    blog
```

Running the `rails new` command will take some time to complete. When it's done, you will have a new directory called `blog` containing the files for our new Ruby on Rails blog application.

Change directory into the `blog` directory:

```
cd blog
```

We can now start our local Rails server using Bundler's `bundle exec` command. This command will run Rails in the context of our application's Gemfile, which will ensure that we are using the correct version of Ruby and Rails and all of the other gems we need for our application.

```
bundle exec rails server
```

We should see output similar to the following:

```
=> Booting Puma
=> Rails 7.0.4.3 application starting in development
=> Run `bin/rails server --help` for more startup options
Puma starting in single mode...
* Puma version: 5.6.5 (ruby 3.2.2-p53) ("Birdie's Version")
```

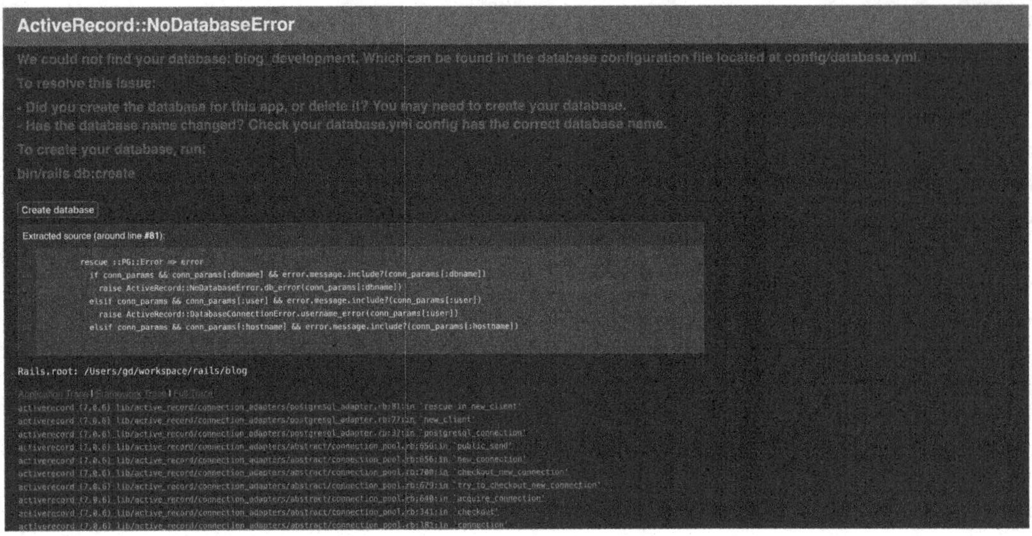

Figure 4-1   The Ruby on Rails error page

```
*   Min threads: 5
*   Max threads: 5
*   Environment: development
*           PID: 11869
* Listening on http://127.0.0.1:3000
* Listening on http://[::1]:3000
Use Ctrl-C to stop
```

If we visit the Rails welcome page at http://127.0.0.1:3000 in our web browser, we should see an error page like the one in Figure 4-1. This is because we haven't created the database named `blog_development` that is defined in our `config/database.yml` file yet. We can fix the error by creating the database using the `rails db:create` command:

```
bundle exec rails db:create
```

Running this command will produce the following output:

```
Created database 'blog_development'
Created database 'blog_test'
```

As seen in the output, we actually get two databases, a development database and a test database. The development database is used for development, and the test database is used strictly for running tests that we will begin writing shortly.

Now if we visit the Rails welcome page at http://127.0.0.1:3000 in our web browser, we should see the Rails welcome page as referenced in Figure 4-2.

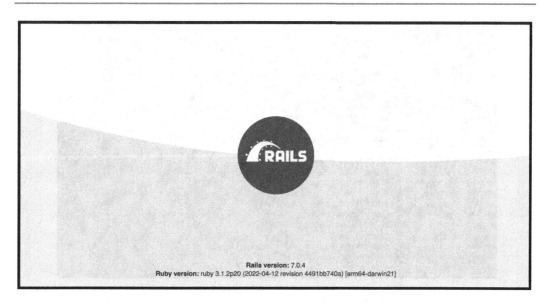

Figure 4-2 The Ruby on Rails welcome page

Running Rails Locally

As mentioned previously, we can run our Ruby on Rails application locally using the `rails server` command along with the `bundle exec` prefix. That's fine for developing Ruby code, but our Rails application will also contain CSS and JavaScript code. There are many different ways to handle CSS and JavaScript in a modern Ruby on Rails application, in both development and production environments.

To ease the burden of managing Ruby, CSS, and JavaScript in our local development environment, the `rails new` command we ran earlier automatically created a `Procfile.dev` file in our application's root directory. This file contains process definitions we need to run our Rails application in our local development.

If we have a look at the `Procfile.dev` file, we will see the following contents:

```
web: unset PORT && env RUBY_DEBUG_OPEN=true bin/rails server
js: yarn build --watch
css: yarn watch:css
```

As is often the case with other files generated by the `rails new` command, this file tends to evolve over time and may appear slightly different in the future. For now, we can see there are three lines, and each line represents a process that will be run when we do something with this file, but how do we run it?

```
06:01:35 web.1  | started with pid 12988
06:01:35 js.1   | started with pid 12989
06:01:35 css.1  | started with pid 12990
06:01:35 css.1  | yarn run v1.22.19
06:01:35 js.1   | yarn run v1.22.19
06:01:35 css.1  | $ sass ./app/assets/stylesheets/application.bootstrap.scss:./app/asset
s/builds/application.css --no-source-map --load-path=node_modules --watch
06:01:35 js.1   | $ esbuild app/javascript/*.* --bundle --sourcemap --outdir=app/assets/
builds --public-path=assets --watch
06:01:35 js.1   | [watch] build finished, watching for changes...
06:01:35 web.1  | => Booting Puma
06:01:35 web.1  | => Rails 7.0.4.3 application starting in development
06:01:35 web.1  | => Run `bin/rails server --help` for more startup options
06:01:36 web.1  | Puma starting in single mode...
06:01:36 web.1  | *  Puma version: 5.6.5 (ruby 3.2.2-p53) ("Birdie's Version")
06:01:36 web.1  | *  Min threads: 5
06:01:36 web.1  | *  Max threads: 5
06:01:36 web.1  | *  Environment: development
06:01:36 web.1  | *          PID: 12988
06:01:36 web.1  | * Listening on http://127.0.0.1:3000
06:01:36 web.1  | * Listening on http://[::1]:3000
06:01:36 web.1  | Use Ctrl-C to stop
06:01:36 css.1  | Sass is watching for changes. Press Ctrl-C to stop.
06:01:36 css.1  |
```

Figure 4-3 Running Rails using foreman

We need to use the `foreman`[10] command to run the processes defined in our `Procfile.dev` file. The `foreman` command can be acquired by installing the `foreman` gem using the command:

```
gem install foreman
```

Before we can actually run `foreman` we need to install `yarn`, a tool that will be used to automate compiling our Javascript and CSS files for us. There are many ways to install `yarn`. I install it from Homebrew using the command:

```
brew install yarn
```

Once we have `foreman` and `yarn` installed, we can run `foreman` using the command:

```
foreman start -f Procfile.dev
```

This will start the `web`, `js`, and `css` processes defined in our `Procfile.dev` file. The output will look similar to Figure 4-3. The `web` process is the Rails server we started earlier. The `js` process is a process that will watch for changes to our JavaScript files and rebuild them as needed. The `css` process is a process that will watch for changes to our CSS files and rebuild them as needed. This will save us a lot of time when developing our Ruby on Rails application.

---

[10]https://github.com/ddollar/foreman

We're almost ready to begin writing our Ruby on Rails blog application in earnest. If you are planning on following along with the rest of the book, you would be wise to commit your code to a version control system at this point.

Summary

In this chapter, we installed the Ruby on Rails framework, along with Bundler and PostgreSQL. We created a new Ruby on Rails application using the `rails new` command. We also learned how to run our Ruby on Rails app in our local development environment using the `foreman` command. Next, we will add RSpec and FactoryBot to our Ruby on Rails application to facilitate writing our first tests.

Setting Up RSpec and FactoryBot

5

RSpec[1] is a testing framework for Ruby. RSpec is available to us as a domain-specific language[2] (DSL) written in Ruby and used to test Ruby code. RSpec tests the behavior of Ruby code and considers itself to be a *"behavior-driven development"* (BDD) framework. RSpec is most widely used for testing Rails applications, but can be used to test any Ruby code.

Ruby on Rails by default comes with the testing framework `Test::Unit`. In the previous chapter when we used the `rails new` command to create our Rails blog application, we added the `--skip-test` option to disable `Test::Unit`. Like *most* Rails developers, we will use RSpec instead of Test::Unit.

Installing RSpec

RSpec is a gem, so we can add it to our Rails blog application by adding it to our `Gemfile` and running the `bundle` command. We want RSpec to be available in both the Rails `development` and `test` environments, so we will add it to both the `:development` and `:test` groups in our Gemfile. The Gemfile addition should then look like this:

```
group :development, :test do
  gem 'rspec-rails'
end
```

Let's save our Gemfile changes and run the `bundle` command:

```
bundle
```

Running the `bundle` command or more verbosely the `bundle install` command will install the `rspec-rails` gem and all of its dependencies. The `bundle` command will also update the `Gemfile.lock` which is used to lock our gems and their dependent gems to specific versions. This

---

[1] https://rspec.info

[2] www.jetbrains.com/mps/concepts/domain-specific-languages/

is important because it ensures we are using the gem versions we mean to in all of our potential Rails environments.

RSpec has now been added to our blog application, but we need one more step to get it working. We need to run the `rails generate rspec:install` command:

```
bundle exec rails generate rspec:install
```

We should see the following output:

```
create  .rspec
create  spec
create  spec/spec_helper.rb
create  spec/rails_helper.rb
```

We can now verify that RSpec is installed and configured by running the `rspec` command:

```
bundle exec rspec
```

We should see the following output:

```
No examples found.

Finished in 0.0002 seconds (files took 0.0351 seconds to
load)
0 examples, 0 failures
```

This output tells us that RSpec is installed and properly configured within our Rails application. We have no tests yet, so RSpec lets us know that it found "*no examples*" to run. In RSpec lingo, an *example* is actually a test, or a spec. We will soon be adding our first RSpec example, so let's move on for now.

Installing FactoryBot

FactoryBot[3] is a Ruby gem that provides a framework and domain-specific language (DSL) for defining and using factories. A FactoryBot factory is a blueprint for creating instances of Ruby classes, or in our use case, Rails ActiveRecord objects. FactoryBot is most widely used for testing Rails applications, but can also be used to test any sort of Ruby code.

But do we really *need* FactoryBot? Can't we just create our test data using Rails and ActiveRecord objects directly?

---

[3] https://github.com/thoughtbot/factory_bot

We could indeed create all of our test data for our blog application using only Rails ActiveRecord objects. For example, we could create a new `user` object using `User.new`, and then we could create a new page object using `Page.new(user:)` that belongs to that user. But this is tedious and error prone, especially if we need to create similar test data many times over or if we need test data with particular traits.

FactoryBot provides more concise and flexible ways to create test data. We can define reusable traits that we can then mix and match to reliably create exactly the test data that we need. We can also choose to only *build* (not create) test data, without actually saving it to our database. This is very useful when we want to test field validation errors, for example.

FactoryBot is of course packaged as a Ruby gem, and there is a Rails-specific version called `factory_bot_rails` that we can use. Let's add it to our application by adding the following line to our `Gemfile` and running the `bundle` command:

```
gem 'factory_bot_rails'
```

We want FactoryBot to be available in all Rails environments, so we will add it outside of any *group* blocks in our Gemfile.

Anytime we add a gem to our Gemfile, we need to then run the `bundle` command to install the new gem and its dependencies. We've done it a few times already, so to save space we won't show the output anymore.

We need to integrate FactoryBot into our Rails application. So let's add it to our `spec/spec_helper.rb` file. Near the top, add the following line:

```
require 'factory_bot_rails'
```

Then, just inside our `RSpec.configure` block, let's add the following:

```
config.include FactoryBot::Syntax::Methods
```

These additions to our RSpec configuration will allow us to use all of the FactoryBot methods in our specs. For example, instead of using the fully qualified "*FactoryBot*" namespace to call the `FactoryBot.create` method, we can instead just use the `create` method directly. This will make our specs cleaner and save us some keystrokes as well.

Another FactoryBot integration we want to take advantage of is the ability for Rails code generators to create factories for our models. To enable this, we need to add the following near the top of our `config/application.rb` file:

```
require 'factory_bot_rails'
```

Further down, inside the same file, let's add this bit of extra configuration inside our `Application` class:

```
config.generators do |g|
  g.test_framework :rspec, fixture: true
  g.fixture_replacement :factory_bot, dir: 'spec/factories'
end
```

This will configure the Rails model generator to use FactoryBot to create factory file stubs whenever we generate a new model. We Ruby developers (especially the author) love saving keystrokes whenever possible. Maybe not as much as Perl developers, but still.

To further facilitate our spec writing, let's install another gem called `shoulda-matchers`.[4] This gem provides a collection of RSpec-compatible one-liners and helpers that will aid us in testing common Rails functionality.

Let's modify our `Gemfile` to add the following line inside the `:test` group:

```
group :test do
  gem 'shoulda-matchers'
end
```

Then let's run the `bundle` command to install the new gem.

To integrate the `shoulda-matchers` gem into RSpec and Rails, we need to add the following configuration into our `spec/rails_helper.rb` file; anywhere near the bottom is fine:

```
Shoulda::Matchers.configure do |config|
  config.integrate do |with|
    with.test_framework :rspec
    with.library :rails
  end
end
```

Debugging

While writing our RSpec tests and Rails application code, we will inevitably encounter errors and other confusing situations where we may not understand exactly what is happening. When we do, we will need to be able to debug our code. We will need to be able to dig deeper into the code's execution and see what is happening at each step. We will need to be able to inspect the variable values and follow different code paths.

---

[4]https://github.com/thoughtbot/shoulda-matchers

The easiest way to debug Ruby code is to use `binding.irb`. This is built into Ruby and allows us to drop into an `irb` session at any point in our code execution. An example call to `binding.irb` may look something like this:

```ruby
# debug.rb

def add(a, b)
  binding.irb
  a + b
end

puts add(1, 2)
```

In our file `debug.rb`, we define a method called `add` that takes two variables and adds them together, returning the result. We then call our method and use `puts` to print the result. We can run this code by executing it with the `ruby` command:

```
ruby debug.rb
```

When our code executes, it will stop at the `binding.irb` line and drop us into an `irb` session. It will look something like this:

```
From: debug.rb @ line 3 :

   1:
   2: def add(a, b)
=> 3:   binding.irb
   4:   a + b
   5: end
   6:
   7: puts add(1, 2)
   8:

irb(main):001:0>
```

We can then inspect our variables and execute any Ruby code we want. When we are done, we can exit the `irb` session by pressing `ctrl-d` or by typing the more verbose `exit` command:

```
  irb(main):001:0> a
=> 1
irb(main):002:0> b
=> 2
irb(main):003:0> a + b
=> 3
irb(main):004:0>
3
```

This is a simple example, but `binding.irb` can be very useful when debugging more complex code too.

There are other more advanced debugging tools available for Ruby; two that I encounter regularly are `pry` and `byebug`. Give them a try and see which one(s) you like best. Over time, I've come to prefer `binding.irb` because I don't have to install or configure anything extra to use it.

Summary

In this chapter, we installed and configured RSpec and FactoryBot, two of the most important tools we will use going forward to create our Rails application's test suite. We will write our tests using RSpec and shoulda-matchers, and we will use FactoryBot to create consistent test data for our tests. We also ran through a simple example showing how to use `binding.irb` to debug our code, just in case we get stuck and need to dig in deeper to figure something out.

Adding Initial Models

6

In this chapter, we will add our first two Rails ActiveRecord models into our blog application. We will start with simple `User` and `Page` models and proceed to grow them, adding more functionality as we go along.

Ruby on Rails is overflowing with *code generators*. Rails code generators create lots of code for us when we run them. We can use the `rails generate` command, for example, to quickly generate a fully namespaced model or a controller with actions and views stubbed and ready for additional development. And since we already have RSpec and FactoryBot installed, we will get appropriately named stub files for those as well. Rails code generators can be huge time savers.

The User Model

In our blog app, a `Page` model will represent a blog post, and a `User` model will represent the person who wrote the blog post. This will allow multiple users to write blog posts if we need that scenario. We will begin by generating the `User` model using the `rails generate` command:

```
bundle exec rails generate model \
                         User \
                         name:string:uniq \
                         email:string:uniq
```

This will generate a *model* as well as a *database migration*, a *factory*, and a *model spec*. The output will look like this:

```
invoke  active_record
create    db/migrate/20221030192603_create_users.rb
create    app/models/user.rb
invoke    rspec
create      spec/models/user_spec.rb
invoke      factory_bot
create        spec/factories/users.rb
```

© The Author(s), under exclusive license to APress Media, LLC, part of Springer Nature 2024   33
G. Donald, *Hands-on Test-Driven Development*,
https://doi.org/10.1007/978-1-4842-9748-3_6

The generated *migration* file will look like this:

```
class CreateUsers < ActiveRecord::Migration[7.0]
  def change
    create_table :users do |t|
      t.string :name
      t.string :email
      t.timestamps
    end
    add_index :users, :name, unique: true
    add_index :users, :email, unique: true
  end
end
```

We're adding the `uniq` option to the `name` and `email` fields to make sure no two users can have the same name or the same email address. This is a common requirement for user accounts, and since we can easily enforce it directly in our database, we should. This will protect us from any other code that creates or modifies user records outside of our Rails app.

In front of our unique database constraints, we will use Rails *model* validations.[1] This will prevent us from showing actual Postgres errors in our web browser. When we try to create a new record with a duplicate name or email address, we will show a nicely formatted error message instead of the entire page being broken.

Let's run our new migrations to create our new database tables:

```
bundle exec rails db:{migrate,test:prepare}
```

This will actually run two commands: first `db:migrate` and then after that `db:test:prepare` will be run. The first will run our migration against our development database, and the second will prepare our test database for use, making sure it matches our development database.

Most of the time after I migrate my database, I run `psql` to connect to my database and check the schema. This is a good way to make sure the migration did what I expected. Let's do that now. We can connect to our development database with the following Rails command:

```
bundle exec rails db
```

Since we're using PostgreSQL, this command will connect us to our `blog_development` database using PostgreSQL's `psql` program. If you're on an underpowered machine, this may take longer than

---

[1] https://guides.rubyonrails.org/active_record_validations.html

you'd like to start up, as it loads the entire Rails codebase. If it's too much to bear, you can always run `psql` directly as shown in the previous chapter:

```
psql blog_development
```

Once we're connected to our database, we can run the `\d` command to see a list of all the tables in our database:

```
blog_development=# \d
                    List of relations
  Schema  |         Name         | Type  | Owner
----------+----------------------+-------+----------
 public   | ar_internal_metadata | table | gd
 public   | pages                | table | gd
 public   | schema_migrations    | table | gd
 public   | users                | table | gd
 (4 rows)
```

As we can see, our `pages` and `users` tables have been created. We can further examine the schema of a given table by running the `\d` command followed by the table name:

```
blog_development=# \d users
```

Have a look and make sure the `users` and `pages` tables match our migrations.

The User Factory

Next, let's improve our new user factory in `spec/factories/users.rb`. Right now, it looks like this:

```
FactoryBot.define do
  factory :user do
    name { "MyString" }
    email { "MyString" }
  end
end
```

Given our unique constraints on our name and email fields, this will fail on the second usage when it tries to create a user record with the same name and email as the first usage. Let's fix that by adding a FactoryBot `sequence` to the `name` and `email` fields:

```
FactoryBot.define do
  factory :user do
    sequence(:name) { |n| "First#{n} Last#{n}" }
    sequence(:email) { |n| "user#{n}@example.com" }
  end
end
```

This will cause the factory to generate name values like "First1 Last1" and "First2 Last2" and email values like "user1@example.com" and "user2@example.com." The `sequence` method takes a field name and a block that will be called each time a new record is created. The block will be passed a sequential number that will be used to generate unique values.

Some software engineers consider sequentially numbering field values to be a sort of anti-pattern, but I think it's a useful option. When we encounter a scenario where we need higher-quality values, we should definitely take the time to create them by hand. For most cases where we just need non-random unique values, a sequential numbering tool is a good way to accomplish that.

Now we're ready to add field validation specs for our name and email fields to our `User` model. Right now, our *User model spec* located in `spec/models/user_spec.rb` looks like this:

```
require 'rails_helper'

RSpec.describe User, type: :model do
  pending "add some examples to (or delete) #{__FILE__}"
end
```

Let's remove the `pending` entry and replace it with a spec to make sure our factory is working as expected:

```
require 'rails_helper'

RSpec.describe User, type: :model do
  let(:user) { build(:user) }

  it 'has a valid factory' do
    expect(user).to be_valid
  end
end
```

This is a very simple spec, but it's a good start. We are using the `build` method from FactoryBot to create a new `User` instance. `build` just creates the instance in memory and doesn't write any data to our database, so it's very fast. We create the `User` instance using RSpec's `let` syntax. `let` is lazily evaluated and, as we'll see later, can come in very handy for making our spec files clean and easy to understand.

Every factory we create should be this easy to instantiate, and adding a spec ensures we don't accidentally break it later. Our spec just checks if our `user` instance is valid using RSpec's `be_*` syntax. Our `expect` statement, as you may have guessed, is expecting our `user` instance to "*be valid.*" If it is not valid, then our spec will fail, and we will know that our factory became broken somehow. It's equivalent to this more verbose version:

```
expect(user.valid?).to eq(true)
```

RSpec's `be_*` syntax is very powerful and can be used to test anything that responds to a boolean query. For example, we can test if a string is empty, like this:

```
expect('').to be_empty
```

Or we can verify something is actually a hash or not:

```
expect({a: 1}).to be_a(Hash)
```

How to Run Specs

We software engineers have different preferences for how we like to run our specs. I like to run my specs in a terminal, so I can see the output and any errors in a large window, with the least amount of scrolling. I may also run my specs inside my code editor from time to time, but this is usually a scenario involving existing specs that I want to quickly verify that I have not broken.

Let's use the `rspec` command to run our new `User` model spec:

```
bundle exec rspec spec/models/user_spec.rb
```

The output will look like this:

```
.

Finished in 0.04421 seconds (files took 0.78106 seconds
to load)
1 example, 0 failures
```

There are two indicators here that our first spec passed. The first is the period (`.`) on the first line. If our spec had failed, we would have got an `F` instead of a period. The second indicator is the *1 example, 0 failures.*

User Model Validations

Now that we can run specs, let's add field validation specs to our `User` model spec file.
We need to first test that our `name` field is present and unique. We can do this with the
`validate_presence_of` and the `validate_uniqueness_of` shoulda-matchers. Let's
add these to our spec file just below the previous spec:

```
describe 'validations' do
  it { is_expected.to validate_presence_of(:name) }
  it { is_expected.to validate_uniqueness_of(:name) }
end
```

I tend to put all my shoulda-matchers and validations near the top of my spec file, but you can organize
your specs however you like. You could add these new specs to the top or to the bottom of your own
file; RSpec does not care about the order when it runs your specs.

When we run our spec, we will get two expected failure messages:

```
1) User validations is expected to validate that :name cannot be
   empty/falsy
    Failure/Error: it { is_expected.to validate_presence_of(:name) }

      Expected User to validate that :name cannot be empty/falsy, but
      this could not be proved.
        After setting :name to ‹""›, the matcher expected the User to
        be invalid, but it was valid instead.

2) User validations is expected to validate that :name is
   case-sensitively unique
    Failure/Error:
      it { is_expected.to validate_uniqueness_of(:name) }

      Expected User to validate that :name is case-sensitively
      unique, but this could not be proved.
        After taking the given User, whose :name is ‹"First2 Last2"›,
        and saving it as the existing record, then making a new User
        and setting its :name to ‹"First2 Last2"› as well, the
        matcher expected the new User to be invalid, but it was valid
        instead.
```

We are using RSpec's `describe` block syntax to group our specs into logical units. First, we have a
validations group, then inside we begin to use RSpec with shoulda-matchers to test individual fields.

To get these two specs to pass, we need to add our missing `name` field validations to our `User`
model. We can do this by adding the following to our `User` model:

```
class User < ApplicationRecord
  validates :name,
            presence: true,
```

```
                uniqueness: true
end
```

This gets our name specs to pass. We can now add specs to test that our email field is also present and unique:

```
it { is_expected.to validate_presence_of(:email) }
it { is_expected.to validate_uniqueness_of(:email) }
```

When we re-run our spec, we get the following output:

```
1) User validations is expected to validate that :email cannot be
   empty/falsy
    Failure/Error:
      it { is_expected.to validate_presence_of(:email) }

      Expected User to validate that :email cannot be empty/falsy,
      but this could not be proved.
        After setting :email to <"">, the matcher expected the User
        to be invalid, but it was valid instead.

2) User validations is expected to validate that :email is
   case-sensitively unique
    Failure/Error:
      it { is_expected.to validate_uniqueness_of(:email) }

      Expected User to validate that :email is case-sensitively
      unique, but this could not be proved.
        After taking the given User, whose :email is
        <"user4@example.com">, and saving it as the existing record,
        then making a new User and setting its :email to
        <"user4@example.com"> as well, the matcher expected the new
        User to be invalid, but it was valid instead.
```

To get these two email specs to pass, we need to add the following to our User model:

```
validates :email,
          presence: true,
          uniqueness: true
```

This gets our email specs to pass.

We can also add some sanity checks to ensure our email address data looks like actual email addresses. How far you take email address validation is up to you. I (used to?) have a Perl book that showed a regular expression to properly validate an email address, and it is more than an entire printed page in length. We're not going to go that far here, but we can add some simple sanity checks to our `describe` validation block:

```
it { is_expected.to_not allow_value('foo@').for(:email) }
it { is_expected.to_not allow_value('@bar.com').for(:email) }
```

When we re-run our spec, we get the expected failure messages:

```
1) User validations is expected not to allow :email to be
   <"foo@">
   Failure/Error:
    it { is_expected.to_not allow_value('foo@').for(:email) }

    After setting :email to <"foo@">, the matcher expected the User
    to be invalid, but it was valid instead.

2) User validations is expected not to allow :email to be
   <"@bar.com">
   Failure/Error:
    it { is_expected.to_not allow_value('@bar.com').for(:email) }

    After setting :email to <"@bar.com">, the matcher expected the
    User to be invalid, but it was valid instead.
```

We can get these two specs passing by adding a `format` validation to our `User` model email validation:

```
validates :email,
          presence: true,
          uniqueness: true,
          format: { with: /\A\S+@\S+\z/ }
```

The content of our `with:` parameter is a regular expression that will validate the format of our email addresses. We use word boundary matchers `\A` and `\z` to ensure the email address does not begin or end with a whitespace character. We use `\S` to match any number of non-whitespace characters, followed by matching the @ symbol. Last we make sure we have some non-whitespace characters after the @ symbol. This is a very simple regular expression, but it will catch a lot of common mistakes made when entering email addresses.

Let's leave our User model as is for now and move on to our Page model.

The Page Model

Let's work on our Page model next. We'll use the `rails generate` command as before:

```
bundle exec rails generate model \
                    Page \
                    user:references \
                    title:string:uniq \
                    slug:string:uniq \
                    summary:text \
                    content:text \
                    published:boolean:index
```

This will generate a Page model as well as a *database migration*, a *factory*, and a *model spec*. The output will look like this:

```
invoke    active_record
create      db/migrate/20221030235303_create_pages.rb
create      app/models/page.rb
invoke      rspec
create        spec/models/page_spec.rb
invoke        factory_bot
create          spec/factories/pages.rb
```

The generated Page migration file needs some work. There are a few things Rails does not currently support with command line–generated database migrations, adding an index to our `created_at` field or setting fields to not be NOT NULL (null: false), for example.

We'll need to manually update our migration to look like this:

```ruby
class CreatePages < ActiveRecord::Migration[7.0]
  def change
    create_table :pages do |t|
      t.references :user, null: false, foreign_key: true
      t.string :title, null: false
      t.string :slug, null: false
      t.text :summary, null: false
      t.text :content, null: false
      t.boolean :published, null: false, default: false
      t.timestamps
    end
    add_index :pages, :title, unique: true
    add_index :pages, :slug, unique: true
    add_index :pages, :published
    add_index :pages, :created_at
```

```
     end
   end
```

Now we can run our new migration to migrate our database:

```
bundle exec rails db:{migrate,test:prepare}
```

Next, let's improve our new page factory in `spec/factories/pages.rb`. Currently, it's using default values and looks like this:

```
FactoryBot.define do
  factory :page do
    user { nil }
    title { 'MyString' }
    slug { 'my-string' }
    summary { 'MyText' }
    content { 'MyText' }
    published { false }
  end
end
```

Let's first add a spec to ensure the `Page` model instances we create with this factory are valid:

```
require 'rails_helper'

RSpec.describe Page, type: :model do
  let(:page) { build(:page) }

  it 'has a valid factory' do
    expect(page).to be_valid
  end
end
```

When we run our `spec/models/page_spec.rb` specs, we see that our factory is not currently creating valid `Page` instances:

```
F

Failures:

1) Page has a valid factory
   Failure/Error: expect(page).to be_valid
     expected #<Page id: nil, user_id: nil, title:
     "MyString", slug: "my-string", summary: "MyText",
```

```
       content: "MyText", published: false, created_at:
       nil, updated_at: nil> to be valid, but got errors:
       User must exist
     # ./spec/models/page_spec.rb:7:in `block (2 levels)
     in <top (required)>'

Finished in 0.05983 seconds (files took 1.08 seconds to
load)
1 example, 1 failure

Failed examples:

rspec ./spec/models/page_spec.rb:6 # Page has a valid
factory
```

It's a big error message, with the important part being the line that says *"User must exist."* We're getting this particular error message because we gave our `Page` model a `belongs_to :user` association via our `user:references` command-line option. This means that every `Page` instance must have a `user_id` field that references a valid `User` instance. We can fix this by updating our `Page` factory to automatically create an associated `User` instance when we use it to create a new `Page` instance:

```
user { create(:user) }
```

Now when we run our specs, we see that it passes.

Next, let's add more specs to our `Page` spec file. Let's add specs to ensure the `Page` model is invalid when the `title` and `content` attributes are not present. We'll also add a spec to ensure our `title` value is unique. We always want an associated user too, and we don't want our database blowing up; we instead want Rails to catch the error before the database does. Let's add the following `Page` model specs:

```
describe 'validations' do
  it { is_expected.to belong_to(:user) }
  it { is_expected.to validate_presence_of(:title) }
  it { is_expected.to validate_uniqueness_of(:title) }
  it { is_expected.to validate_presence_of(:content) }
end
```

When we run our `Page` spec file, we see that we have a new failure:

```
...F.

Failures:

  1) Page validations is expected to validate that :title
```

```
        is case-sensitively unique
        Failure/Error: it { is_expected.to
        validate_uniqueness_of(:title) }

        Shoulda::Matchers::ActiveRecord::
        ValidateUniquenessOfMatcher::ExistingRecordInvalid:
          validate_uniqueness_of works by matching a new
          record against an existing record. If there is no
          existing record, it will create one using the
          record you provide.

          While doing this, the following error was raised:

            PG::NotNullViolation: ERROR:  null value in
            column "user_id" of relation "pages" violates
            not-null constraint
            DETAIL:  Failing row contains (1, null, null,
            null, null, null, f, 2022-11-02 00:27:42.12824,
            2022-11-02 00:27:42.12824).

          The best way to fix this is to provide the
          matcher with a record where any required
          attributes are filled in with valid values
          beforehand.
        # ./spec/models/page_spec.rb:14:in `block (3
        levels) in <top (required)>'
        # ------------------
        # --- Caused by: ---
        # PG::NotNullViolation:
        #   ERROR:  null value in column "user_id" of
        #   relation "pages" violates not-null constraint
        #   DETAIL:  Failing row contains (1, null, null,
        #   null, null, null, f, 2022-11-02 00:27:42.12824,
        #   2022-11-02 00:27:42.12824).
        #   ./spec/models/page_spec.rb:14:in `block (3
        #   levels) in <top (required)>'

Finished in 0.1452 seconds (files took 0.87346 seconds to load)
5 examples, 1 failure

Failed examples:

rspec ./spec/models/page_spec.rb:14 # Page validations is
expected to validate that :title is case-sensitively unique
```

This error message seems to be saying Postgres is preventing us from adding a new `Page` instance without a `user_id` field, as previously discussed. But the weird part is it's actually failing on the spec for requiring a unique `title`.

What's going on here? Is there some implied `Page` record being created?

RSpec's "subject"

When we're using RSpec, each individual spec file has a sort of "*magic*" variable called `"subject"`. This variable is automatically set based on our spec file's name and what type of spec it is. In our case, we're testing our `Page` model, so our implied `subject` variable is set to a new `Page` instance.

Our shoulda-matchers use RSpec's implied `subject` variable to perform the validation. So when we're testing the uniqueness of our `title` value in a shoulda-matcher, we're actually testing the uniqueness of our `title` value on the implied `subject`.

In our case, RSpec is by default building a new instance of `Page` without a `user_id` field. It just doesn't know any better unless we tell it to do something different. We can fix our spec failure by telling RSpec what we actually want for a `subject` in our spec file. One option is to do something like this:

```
describe 'validations' do
  subject { build(:page) }
  it { is_expected.to belong_to(:user) }
  it { is_expected.to validate_presence_of(:title) }
  it { is_expected.to validate_uniqueness_of(:title) }
  it { is_expected.to validate_presence_of(:content) }
end
```

So just inside our one `describe` block, we're telling RSpec to use our own custom `subject` instead of the implied one. This works, but it's a bit of a pain to have to do this for every `describe` block.

Another option could be to reuse the `page` we're already building at the top of our spec:

```
subject { page }
```

This is an improvement, but it's still not great because it's redundant.

The solution I prefer is to define my `subject` at the top of my spec file, so my attention is immediately drawn to it whenever I open the file:

```
subject { build(:page) }
```

Now when we're reading our spec file, we can immediately see what our `subject` is for all of our specs. Let's do a bit of cleanup and have our `Page` spec look like this:

```
require 'rails_helper'

RSpec.describe Page, type: :model do
  subject { build(:page) }

  describe 'validations' do
```

```
    it { is_expected.to belong_to(:user) }
    it { is_expected.to be_valid }
    it { is_expected.to validate_presence_of(:title) }
    it { is_expected.to validate_uniqueness_of(:title) }
    it { is_expected.to validate_presence_of(:content) }
  end
end
```

There's not much harm in redefining our subject in any subsequent describe block, as needed, but we should try to have a clean and simple default subject at the top of each spec file if possible.

Now that our code is better organized and we have become experts on RSpec's subject variable, let's get our failing specs passing by adding our currently missing model validations to our Page model:

```
class Page < ApplicationRecord
  belongs_to :user

  validates :title,
            presence: true,
            uniqueness: true

  validates :content,
            presence: true
end
```

Now our Page specs are passing.

FactoryBot "build" vs. "create"

There is the cost of a database write if our FactoryBot build call is instead a call to create. We should keep that in mind and always consider using build unless we actually need to persist the record in our database. We can even default to using build and then call .save on our subject as needed. It's a great way to make sure we're only persisting records when we actually need to.

Writing records to our database is often the slowest part of a spec. It's best to avoid doing it whenever possible.

The Page slug

In web development, we should try to use human-friendly URLs for a given resource. Instead of using the URL http://example.com/pages/1, or the even uglier http://example.com/pages?id=1, we should build our app to use beautiful URLs such as http://example.com/pages/first-page.

The "*first-page*" part, at the end of the URL, is called the slug. I honestly do not know why it's called that, but I've heard it called that so many times, I now call it that too.

It would be unnecessary extra work to create the URL-friendly slug every time we make a page, and since we're already making a title that is very similar, we should just use the title to generate the `slug` value for us. If we do it correctly, we can even maintain our `slug` uniqueness validation along the way.

So we want to provide a `title` with any sort of a value and then take that value and make it all lowercase, with no spaces, and using dashes as word delimiters. Let's first capture our idea in a new spec.

Let's provide a complicated `title` value and then make sure the `slug` ends up becoming what we expect:

```
describe '#slug' do
  let(:page) { create(:page, title: '--Foo Bar! _ 87 --') }

  it 'is generated from the title' do
    expect(page.slug).to eq('foo-bar-87')
  end
end
```

When we run this spec, we get the failure:

```
1) Page#slug is generated from the title
Failure/Error: expect(page.slug).to eq('foo-bar-87')

  expected: "foo-bar-87"
       got: "my-string"
```

The "my-string" is still the default value for the `slug` field in our factory. Let's remove it, knowing that our subject uses the FactoryBot `build` method and that we need some sort of value for our shoulda-matcher to work. As expected, we get a different failure message:

```
ActiveRecord::NotNullViolation:
  PG::NotNullViolation: ERROR:  null value in column "slug" of
  relation "pages" violates not-null constraint
```

It's telling us that the `slug` field is not allowed to be null, and remembering back to our database migration for our `pages` table, that's correct behavior. We need to update our `Page` model to make our `slug` value for us, automatically.

Rails provides "*callbacks*" in the ActiveRecord class. A callback is a method that is called at a particular point in the life cycle of an ActiveRecord object. We can use a callback to generate our `slug` for us. We'll use the `before_validation` callback to generate our `slug` just before we save the record to our database. There's a `before_save` callback, but we want to generate our `slug` before Rails validates the record, so it would actually fire too late for our particular use case, so we will user `before_validation`.

```
class Page < ApplicationRecord
```

```
# previously added code omitted for brevity

before_validation :make_slug

private

def make_slug
  self.slug = title
                .downcase
                .gsub(/[_ ]/, '-')
                .gsub(/[^-a-z0-9+]/, '')
                .gsub(/-{2,}/, '-')
                .gsub(/^-/, '')
                .chomp('-')
  end
end
```

That's a lot of gsub calls, so let's run through it all. First, we make the title lowercase by calling downcase. Then we replace all spaces and underscores with dashes, giving them special treatment early on since spaces and underscores are typical word delimiters. Then we remove any characters that are not dashes, lowercase letters, or numbers. Then we remove any duplicate dashes. Finally, we remove any dashes at the beginning and end of the string. That's a lot of work to make a slug, but if you re-run our spec, you can see that it works and that our spec is now passing.

Page Factory

Before we go much further, let's polish our Page factory a bit. We can use FactoryBot sequences to generate different but predictable (not random) data for our Page data:

```
FactoryBot.define do
  factory :page do
    user { create(:user) }
    sequence(:title) { |n| "Page Title #{n}" }
    sequence(:slug) { |n| "page-title-#{n}" }
    sequence(:summary) { |n| "<p>Page summary goes here #{n}</p>" }
    sequence(:content) { |n| "<p>Page content goes here #{n}</p>" }
    created_at { Time.zone.now }
    published { false }
  end
end
```

Random Test Data

Some software engineers recommend using random data in their factories, for example, the Faker gem, but I strongly advise against doing that, especially if the randomly generated factory data is used in specs. Random test data causes random spec failures, which are often difficult and time-consuming to debug. These random test failures will at some point become blockers for important things like Friday afternoon production deployments!

The first thing I do when I work on a randomly failing spec is to begin to look for where some bits of random data are coming into the picture, on purpose or by accident. Sometimes, things you don't think will ever be random end up becoming random when you least expect it. Consider `Time.zone.now` and how it works on your local development machine where you probably have a local time zone set versus how it will work in a CI environment where the time zone is probably set to UTC. Then imagine your test suite running late in the evening where it becomes "tomorrow" compared to your local machine that still thinks it's "today." To complicate debugging efforts further, imagine some of your team members are on the other side of the planet from you.

I do not use the term "flakey spec" when describing a randomly failing spec. That sort of terminology has an underlying meaning of "I don't really know why this spec is failing and I'd rather imply it's RSpec's fault instead of spending the time to figure it out." Instead, I advise using the words "randomly failing spec" which is encouragement to spend the time to figure out why it's random.

Remember, RSpec is not a fuzzing tool, it's an acceptance testing framework. Acceptance testing means putting in known inputs and expecting to get back predictable outputs. Always steer clear of random data in your factories and specs.

Final Thoughts on Model Validations

This chapter was a whirlwind tour of Rails model validations. We covered a lot of small topics and saw how they fit together in a practical hands-on way. We used tools that actual Ruby software engineers use every day. We leaned heavily on FactoryBot and will continue to do so throughout the book. Repeatability is important, especially when it comes to writing specs.

Before we close out the chapter, let's take a moment for some cleanup.

User Spec Cleanup

A few sections ago, we became RSpec `subject` experts, so let's now clean up our `User` spec:

```
require 'rails_helper'

RSpec.describe User, type: :model do
  subject { build(:user) }

  describe 'validations' do
    it { is_expected.to be_valid }
    it { is_expected.to validate_presence_of(:name) }
    it { is_expected.to validate_uniqueness_of(:name) }
    it { is_expected.to validate_presence_of(:email) }
    it { is_expected.to validate_uniqueness_of(:email) }
    it { is_expected.to allow_value('foo@bar.com').for(:email) }
    it { is_expected.to_not allow_value('@bar.com').for(:email) }
    it { is_expected.to_not allow_value('foo@').for(:email) }
  end
end
```

That's a lot cleaner and easier to read, and we're getting a lot of value out of such a small amount of code.

Advice on Writing Too Many Specs

In our blog application, we won't pursue writing every single spec that is automatically generated for us. These automatically generated spec files are mostly harmless to remain empty, and we will eventually delete them when we don't want them hanging around anymore. I wanted to take a moment to explain why we won't be filling in every spec file that is generated for us.

It's not that writing every single spec we can is a horrible world-ending idea, it's that we will be writing enough specs to provide more than ample cover of any logic we might create.

Undoubtedly, you will have, or will soon have, your own preferences for what specs you want to write for your own apps. My preferences have evolved, as my experience grew. The best way to grow this level of experience is to practice test-driven development. Having a failing test, failing exactly like you expect it to fail, is the best way to learn how to write the best code possible, to get that spec to pass.

Summary

In this chapter, we learned about shoulda-matchers and Rails model validations and how to use them to ensure our data is valid before it gets saved to our database. I also gave some experienced advice on how using random data often causes random test failures. Next, we're going to jump headfirst into Rails routes and controllers while creating our application's homepage.

Creating Pages

7

It may be surprising to make it all the way to this chapter without having written any HTML yet; we are creating a web application after all! We've been doing a lot of preparation, making sure we get off to a solid start. Rest assured, it's now time to get down to business. In this chapter, we'll create our homepage, which will be the first page that users see when they visit our site.

We'll start by writing a system spec for our homepage and learn about *Capybara*,[1] a tool that facilitates web browser testing from inside our system specs.

System Specs

A system spec is a spec that simulates a user interacting with our application directly. It will do things exactly as the user would, things such as visiting URLs, filling out forms, and clicking buttons and links.

But why would we use a system spec when we could instead use a controller spec or a request spec? The two test types both make HTTP requests after all. The biggest reason is JavaScript. Request specs are great for testing the behavior of our application at the HTTP request/response level, and controller specs are great for testing the behavior of our Rails application at the routing/controller level, but neither of these approaches will exercise our JavaScript.

Testing Our Homepage

Let's start by writing a simple system spec for our homepage. It will require significant effort to get it to pass, but that's how TDD works! We'll start with adding a new spec file into our `spec/system` directory. Let's add this to a file named `home_spec.rb`:

```
require 'rails_helper'

RSpec.describe 'Home' do
  it 'renders homepage' do
    visit root_path
```

---

[1] http://teamcapybara.github.io/capybara/

© The Author(s), under exclusive license to APress Media, LLC, part of Springer Nature 2024
G. Donald, *Hands-on Test-Driven Development*,
https://doi.org/10.1007/978-1-4842-9748-3_7

```
    within 'header' do
      expect(page).to have_link 'My Blog'
    end
  end
end
```

When we run our new system spec with the command:

```
bundle exec rspec spec/system/home_spec.rb
```

we get a lot of output, with the important part of the error message near the end:

```
Gem::LoadError:
  capybara is not part of the bundle. Add it to your Gemfile.
# ./spec/system/home_spec.rb:3:in `<top (required)>'
```

There's nothing better than an error message telling us exactly what we need to do to fix it! Let's add capybara to our Gemfile, in our :test group:

```
group :test do
  gem 'capybara'
end
```

Then, as before, we need to run bundle to install our new gem. Some Ruby developers like to run bundle install instead of just bundle, but I prefer less typing anytime I'm given the choice.

Now that we have capybara installed, let's run our new system spec again. Our previous error message is gone, but we have a new one:

```
Gem::LoadError:
selenium-webdriver is not part of the bundle. Add it to your Gemfile.
```

We are presented with another highly informative error message; we need the selenium-webdriver. But before we add it to our Gemfile, let's consider a better option. There is a gem called webdrivers that will automatically install the latest version of selenium-webdriver for us, as well as other webdrivers for many different web browsers. Let's add it to our Gemfile and run bundle:

```
group :test do
  gem 'webdrivers'
end
```

Keep in mind there may be other gems in the `:test` group of our Gemfile. To save space, I'm not going to show them all every time we make a modification.

Now that we have `webdrivers` installed, let's run our spec again. This time, we get a different error message:

```
1) Home renders homepage
   Failure/Error: visit root_path

NameError:
  undefined local variable or method `root_path' for
  #<RSpec::ExampleGroups::Home "renders homepage"
  (./spec/system/home_spec.rb:4)>
# ./spec/system/home_spec.rb:5:in `block (2 levels) in <top
(required)>'
```

This error message may seem cryptic, but it just means that we're missing a Rails route. In Rails, the `root_path` is the path for the root URL of our application. As this is a brand-new Rails application, our `root_path` simply has not been defined yet. If we open up `config/routes.rb`, we can see the `root` method is still commented out:

```
# root "articles#index"
```

Let's uncomment it and add a route for our homepage, so our routes file looks like this:

```
Rails.application.routes.draw do
  root 'home#index'
end
```

The argument we're passing to the `root` method is the name of a controller and action we will use for our homepage, separated with a # symbol.

When we call up the root URL of our application, Rails will look for a controller class named `Home` that contains an action named `index`. If it finds them, it will execute the action and do whatever it says to do. If it doesn't find them, it will throw an error, just like we'll see if we now run our spec again (you may have to scroll up a bit to see this exact error message):

```
1) Home renders homepage
   Failure/Error: raise MissingController.new(error.message,
   error.name)

   ActionController::RoutingError:
     uninitialized constant HomeController
```

Our practice of test-driven development is really paying off. It continues to guide us with making changes, only as needed, to get our spec to pass. At this point, we're being guided to create our Home controller and index action. Let's create them now using a Rails generator:

```
bundle exec rails generate controller home index
```

A Quick Confession

I'm going to confess something here. I don't type that full bundle exec command very often. I've been typing it out up until now because it's the proper way to use bundler with a Rails application. The truth is I have an alias in my .zshrc file that looks like this:

```
alias be='bundle exec'
```

In addition to my alias, Rails itself has an internal alias for the generate portion of the command, the letter g. So what I usually type out for that command is this:

```
be rails g controller home index
```

This gives me the same result as if I have typed out the longer command. The Rails g alias also works for other generators like model. From now on, we'll use the shorter commands.

After we run our generate command, we get our new controller and our new controller action, and some other new files as well:

```
create  app/controllers/home_controller.rb
 route  get 'home/index'
invoke  erb
create    app/views/home
create    app/views/home/index.html.erb
invoke  rspec
create    spec/requests/home_spec.rb
create    spec/views/home
create    spec/views/home/index.html.erb_spec.rb
invoke  helper
create    app/helpers/home_helper.rb
invoke    rspec
create      spec/helpers/home_helper_spec.rb
```

We can ignore most of these files for now, but one change that just occurred inside our `config/routes.rb` file is the addition of a new `get` route:

```
get 'home/index'
```

Rails is being helpful, and normally we may very well want the new route addition, but since we already have a route for our `root_path`, we don't actually need it. Let's remove it.

Let's run our spec again. Our previous error appears to be fixed, and we're getting a new error message:

```
1) Home renders homepage
    Failure/Error:
      within 'header' do
        expect(page).to have_link 'My Blog'
      end

    Capybara::ElementNotFound:
      Unable to find css "header"
```

It looks like it's finally time to write some HTML, but where do we write it?

Rails View Templates

In Rails, the files that contain our HTML that gets rendered to our browser are called "*views*" or "*view templates*." In our Rails application, we're using the default template engine "*ERB*," which stands for "*Embedded Ruby*." ERB is a templating language that allows us to embed Ruby code directly inside our HTML code, using a special template syntax. This is very useful because it allows us to use Ruby to dynamically generate HTML. For example, we can use Ruby to generate HTML that is different for each user of our application.

In Rails, an example block of ERB template code might look like this:

```erb
<% if user_signed_in? %>
  <p>Welcome back, <%= current_user.name %></p>
<% else %>
  <p>Welcome to our site!</p>
<% end %>
```

The first line of this code is just a plain old Ruby `if` statement. The magic is that it is wrapped with ERB opening and closing brackets. This allows us to embed Ruby code directly in our HTML code. The `if` condition checks to see if the current user is signed in. If the user is signed in, the next line of code will be evaluated, and the result will be inserted into the HTML, welcoming them back to our website by name. Notice the different `<%=` starting bracket syntax; it contains an = symbol unlike the other brackets surrounding our `if` code. We use this version of the opening ERB bracket when we want to insert something into our HTML.

Following the `if` is an `else` condition with contents that will be evaluated if the user is *not* signed in. The last line of code is a closing `end` statement that ends the `if`/`else` conditions.

To explain it another way, ERB is just Ruby code that gets evaluated and inserted into our HTML. Outside of an ERB template, the preceding code is equivalent to this:

```
if user_signed_in?
  puts "<p>Welcome back, #{current_user.name}</p>"
else
  puts '<p>Welcome to our site!</p>'
end
```

In this example, our `<%= current_user.name %>` example code is equivalent to our `#{current_user.name}` code; the evaluation delimiters are just different from regular Ruby code to ERB code.

It's easy to get used to ERB syntax. It's just Ruby code with some special syntax that allows it to work inside of and with HTML. I can promise you that most of your ERB template debugging time will be spent on missing = symbols however; at least this is the case for me.

There are other template engines available for Ruby and Rails. I've worked with HAML[2] on several Rails projects, and I've heard good things about Slim.[3] Give them a try if you're interested.

Back to our failing spec. Our spec is failing because it can't find the `<header>` element in our template. We need to create that element, but where? I can think of three possible places to put our HTML code:

1. `app/views/home/index.html.erb`
2. `app/views/layouts/application.html.erb`
3. In a new partial file that we share between our views

As you might have guessed, the third option is the best option. But why?

Our blog header will need to appear on every public page of our application, so we should put it in a partial file that we can render it inside our `app/views/layouts/application.html.erb` file. If we put our code in the `app/views/home/index.html.erb` file, we would end up having duplicate code for every page of our application that needs a header. This is something we want to avoid since changing it would then require us to edit many files instead of just one.

Putting our code in our `app/views/layouts/application.html.erb` file would not be horrible, but this file can become very large and difficult to manage if we put too much code into it. It's better to keep our layout files small and use partials to represent the logical sections of our layout.

---

[2] https://haml.info/
[3] https://slim-template.github.io/

Let's create a new directory named `app/view/shared` and add a new partial file called `_header.html.erb` in there:

```
<header>
  <%= link_to 'My Blog', root_path %>
</header>
```

Notice how our header file's filename starts with an underscore. This is a Rails convention that tells Rails this file is a partial file. We can render this partial file in other templates by using the filename without the underscore. For example, we can render this partial in our `app/views/layouts/application.html.erb` file using the following line of code:

```
<%= render 'shared/header' %>
```

Rails looks in our `app/views` directory for templates by default, so we don't need to specify that directory path in our `render` method call. We just need to specify the path to the partial file relative to our `app/views` directly, which in this case is `shared/header`.

Now that we are Rails partial template experts, we can proceed with rendering our partial in our `app/views/layouts/application.html.erb` layout file by adding the following code just inside our opening `<body>` tag:

```
<body>
  <%= render 'shared/header' %>
  <%= yield %>
</body>
```

The `render` method is a Rails helper method that will render the partial file. The `yield` method is a special method that will render the contents of the current view template. These two concepts will become more clear as we continue to add more partial templates.

Let's run our spec again. This time, it passes! We've successfully rendered our `header` partial in our application layout.

```
.

Finished in 1.51 seconds (files took 1.11 seconds to load)
1 example, 0 failures
```

Configuring Selenium

When we run our new system spec, we can visibly see a browser window open and close as the spec runs. But what if it's not the browser we wanted? What if we want to use "*headless mode*" sometimes but maybe not always? What if we're on our CI server and we can **only** use headless mode?

The answers to these questions are all about configuration. We can configure Capybara to use different drivers for different environments or different environment variables. We can also configure Capybara to use different headless modes for different drivers. It's all about what we decide we need for our application.

For our blog application, we're going to use Chrome as our Capybara-configured browser, and we'll configure a way to run our specs in headless mode whenever we want to.

In our `spec/rails_helper.rb` file, we can configure Capybara. We need to work inside the `RSpec.configure` block. Let's add a new block of code there:

```
config.before(:each, type: :system) do
  driver = :selenium_chrome_headless
  driver = :selenium_chrome if ENV['SHOW_CHROME']
  driven_by(driver)
end
```

This lets us run our spec in headless mode by default, but we can also run it with a visible Chrome browser by setting the `SHOW_CHROME` environment variable on our command line.

Let's run our spec again. This time, we will not see a browser window open:

```
be rspec spec/system/home_spec.rb
```

And then if we use our new `SHOW_CHROME` environment variable, we *will* see a browser window open:

```
SHOW_CHROME=1 be rspec spec/system/home_spec.rb
```

I like this approach because it lets me run my specs in headless mode by default during local development, as well as on my CI server. But if I need to see the browser, for whatever reason, I can easily do that by temporarily setting the environment variable.

Displaying Page Summaries

Continuing development of our blog application's homepage, next we're going to add a list of blog post summaries. We'll start by writing a failing spec for this new functionality. Since we're still working on our homepage, we can continue to use the same spec file. Let's check for a new `article` element in our spec:

```
require 'rails_helper'

RSpec.describe 'Home' do
  it 'renders homepage' do
    create(:page)
```

```
      visit root_path

      within 'header' do
        expect(page).to have_link 'My Blog'
      end

      articles = find_all('article')
      expect(articles.size).to eq(1)

      within articles.first do
        expect(page).to have_css('h2', text: Page.last.title)
      end
    end
  end
```

We're using Capybara's `find_all` method to find all of our `<article>` elements on the page. We're then checking that there is only one `article` element. Next, we use Capybara's `within` method to scope our expectations down to the first `article` element and check that it has an `h2` element with the text of the last `Page` record's `title` attribute.

Using `.last` here is a very common pattern found in specs. It allows us to locate and reference the last record we added to our database without having to know the ID of that record. This is very helpful since the ID of the last record will change every time we re-run our spec. Our `pages` table's ID column is an auto-incrementing integer generated from our database sequence, so the ID of the last record will always be changing to be one greater than the ID of the previous record.

Let's run our spec and see it fail:

```
1) Home renders homepage
     Failure/Error: expect(articles.size).to eq(1)

       expected: 1
            got: 0
```

It seems like the fix might be as simple as adding a new `Page` record to our database and displaying that on the page. But do we want to show all posts? What about the `published` attribute in our `Page` model? We've made no consideration for its usage yet.

Published vs. Unpublished Pages

Not all `Pages` are equal. Some are ready to be published and some need more work and are not. We need the concept of an unpublished `Page` for several important reasons:

1. We want to be able to continue working on a page as many times as required before considering it complete and ready for anyone to read.
2. We don't want to show incomplete or unfinished pages to search engines.
3. We want to be able to retire old pages and remove them from our blog.

Recalling back to when we made our database migration for our pages table, we defaulted our `published` field to `false`. We even took things a step further and had our `Page` factory also default our `published` field to false. This means that when we create a new `Page` record, it will not be `published` by default, with no effort from us or from our code.

All that said, we still need a way to display only published pages. In Rails, we can use the `scope`[4] method to define a named scope on our `Page` model that queries our database for published pages only. Let's add a new model spec for our published scope idea:

```
describe 'scopes' do
  describe '.published' do
    let(:page1) { create(:page, :published) }
    let(:page2) { create(:page) }

    before do
      [page1, page2]
    end

    it 'returns only published pages' do
      expect(Page.published).to eq([page1])
    end
  end
end
```

We're using the `let` method to define two `Page` records. Per our database default, our Pages are unpublished unless we explicitly say otherwise. In our spec, our `page1` instance will be published, while our other `page2` instance will be defaulting to unpublished.

RSpec `let`s are lazily evaluated, so we use the `before` block to create both records in our database before our spec runs. We then add a `describe` block to define our `.published` scope and use the `it` block to check that it returns only the one published `Page` record.

Let's run our spec and see it fail:

```
1) Page scopes .published returns published pages
    Failure/Error: let(:page1) { create(:page, :published) }

    KeyError:
      Trait not registered: "published"
```

We're getting a `KeyError` because we haven't defined a `published` trait in our `Page` factory yet. Let's add that now inside our `factory` block:

```
trait :published do
  published { true }
end
```

---

[4]https://guides.rubyonrails.org/active_record_querying.html#scopes

Let's run our spec again:

```
1) Page scopes .published returns published pages
   Failure/Error: expect(Page.published).to eq([page1])

   NoMethodError:
     undefined method `published' for Page:Class
```

Now we're getting a `NoMethodError` because we haven't defined our `.published` scope yet in our `Page` model class. Let's add that now:

```
scope :published, -> { where(published: true) }
```

Now our new scope spec passes.

Rails scopes are a great way to encapsulate common database queries. We can use them anywhere in our code including inside our controller actions. Let's now use our new `.published` scope.

Displaying Published Pages

To make our posts available to our view, we need to add an instance variable to our `HomeController#index` action. We'll call it `@posts` and assign it to the result of calling our new `.published` scope:

```
def index
  @pages = Page.published
end
```

We can now use our new instance variable in `home/index.html.erb` to display a list of our pages using the page titles:

```erb
<% @pages.each do |page| %>
  <article>
    <h2><%= page.title %></h2>
  </article>
<% end %>
```

Now we just need to go back and update our homepage spec to create a published page; let's add our new `published` trait to our `create(:page)` call:

```
create(:page, :published)
```

That should do it. Let's run our spec and see it pass.

Page Summary Ordering

We've got our homepage displaying our published pages, but they're not necessarily in the correct order. We want our most recent posts to be displayed first, followed by older posts. We can use ActiveRecord's order method to specify the order we want our posts to be displayed, but we want to add it as a scope so it's cleaner and simpler to use. Let's add a new Page model spec file spec/models/page_spec.rb to test our new model scope inside our describe 'scopes' block:

```
describe '.ordered' do
  let(:page1) { create(:page, created_at: 2.days.ago) }
  let(:page2) { create(:page, created_at: 1.day.ago) }

  before do
    [page1, page2]
  end

  it 'returns ordered pages' do
    expect(Page.ordered).to eq([page2, page1])
  end
end
```

We're using let to define two Page records. One is created two days ago, and the other is created one day ago. RSpec lets are lazily evaluated, so we use the before block to create both records in our database. We're creating our new Page records in the opposite order that we expect our scope to order results; this provides additional confidence that our spec won't pass by accident. Running our spec, we get the failure:

```
1) Page scopes .ordered returns ordered pages
Failure/Error: expect(Page.ordered).to eq([page2, page1])

NoMethodError:
  undefined method `ordered' for Page:Class
```

The simplest thing we can do to make progress on our failing spec is to add an empty .ordered scope to our Page model:

```
scope :ordered, -> {}
```

Running our spec again, we get a different failure:

```
1) Page scopes .ordered returns ordered pages
   Failure/Error: expect(Page.ordered).to eq([page2, page1])
     expected: [#<Page id: 642, user_id: 898, title: "Charisma ...
          got: #<ActiveRecord::Relation [#<Page id: 641, ...
```

We can see just from looking at the ids in the failure message that our scope isn't ordering our results correctly. We can fix that by implementing the body of our `.ordered` scope:

```
scope :ordered, -> { order(created_at: :desc) }
```

Running our spec again, we see it passes. We can now use our new `.ordered` scope in our `HomeController#index` action:

```
def index
  @pages = Page.published.ordered
end
```

Happy Paths and System Specs

System specs are not cheap in terms of CPU and memory usage. They spawn some sort of a web client (usually a headless browser) and run our specs against it. As a result, system specs are slower and more resource intensive than any other kind of spec we can write. Being thoughtful software engineers, we do not want to exhaust our limited system resources by running unnecessary system specs.

But what makes a system spec unnecessary?

In general, unnecessary system specs fall into a few categories:

1. Redundant
2. Negative
3. Impossible

For example, we may have a spec that tests that a user can log in successfully. That's a great reason for the system spec to exist. But we don't then also need another system spec that tests that a user *cannot* log in successfully. We can trust that if we somehow break the ability for a user to log in, our original login system spec will fail, and we will realize our mistake. We call the former spec the "*happy path*" and the latter the "*sad*" or "*unhappy*" path.

Do not confuse the *unhappy* path with feature logic. For example, we may have a feature where the user fills out a form and submits it. If the form is invalid, we want to display an error message to the user. That sounds like a feature requirement that we should definitely test. What we should not test is that the error message does not display when the form submission is valid.

We want to keep our system specs focused on the *happy* path and avoid testing anything that is not a feature requirement. We should also do our best to create the smallest possible system spec with the fewest database interactions possible. This will help us keep our system specs fast and efficient.

Sometimes, we will find that something we first think to put in a system spec can instead be placed in a view spec or a request spec. This is definitely a "*right tool for the job*" scenario. It's our job as software engineers to choose the right tool for the job. Let's do our jobs!

Displaying a Single Page

Next, we want to be able to display a single page. Let's create a new system spec file named `spec/system/page_spec.rb` and add a new spec for our single page:

Custom Routing

```
require 'rails_helper'

RSpec.describe 'Pages' do
  let(:my_page) { create(:page, :published) }

  it 'renders page' do
    visit page_path(slug: my_page.slug)

    article = find('article')

    within article do
      expect(page).to have_css('h2', text: my_page.title)
    end
  end
end
```

We're again using the FactoryBot `create` method to create a published page. We then use Capybara's `visit` method to visit the page's URL. Next, we use the `find` method to find our `article` element on the page. After that, we use the `within` method to scope our expectations to only the `article` element and its contents. Finally, we use the `have_css` matcher to check that the `article` element contains an h2 element with the text of the page's title.

   This spec will give us plenty to do. Let's work through the failures. Running our spec will give us our first failure:

```
1) Pages renders page
   Failure/Error: visit page_path(slug: my_page.slug)

   NoMethodError:
     undefined method `page_path' for #<RSpec::ExampleGroups::Pages
     "renders page" (./spec/system/page_spec.rb:6)>
```

We're getting a `NoMethodError` because we don't have a `page_path` route yet. Let's modify our `config/routes.rb` file to add a route for our pages:

```
get 'page/:slug',
    to: 'pages#show',
    slug: /[-a-z0-9+]*/,
    as: :page
```

This is a custom route that aids us in creating our beautiful URLs we discussed before. The :slug value must match our regular expression /[-a-z0-9+]*/, and then when it does, our request is sent to our show action in our Pages controller. Re-running our spec shows us our next failure:

```
1) Pages renders page
   Failure/Error: raise MissingController.new(error.message,
   error.name)

   ActionController::RoutingError:
     uninitialized constant PagesController
```

Not surprising, we have not created our PagesController yet. Let's create it and add a #show action as well:

```
be rails g controller pages show
```

This moves us to our next spec failure:

```
1) Pages renders page
   Failure/Error: article = find('article')

   Capybara::ElementNotFound:
     Unable to find css "article"
```

Having an empty #show action is not enough to make our spec pass. We need to query our database for the page we want to display and then set that result as an instance variable, for use in our view template. Let's add a #find_by query to our #show action:

```
class PagesController < ApplicationController
  def show
    @page = Page.published.find_by(slug: params[:slug])
  end
end
```

In addition to our #find_by query, we need to also make sure that we only find and return published pages. We can do that by chaining our #find_by query to our #published scope.

This will give us a @page instance variable that we can use in our view:

```
<article>
  <h2><%= @page.title %></h2>
</article>
```

Our spec should now pass. Let's run it and see:

```
be rspec spec/system/page_spec.rb
```

```
.

Finished in 1.16 seconds (files took 1.07 seconds to load)
1 example, 0 failures
```

Broken Specs and Warnings

We used Rails code generators to generate our PagesController and our HomeController, and along the way matching request specs were also generated for us. If we run RSpec against our generated request specs, we will see that we have some failures. The first one is in our spec/requests/home_spec.rb file:

```
1) Homes GET /index returns http success
   Failure/Error: get "/home/index"

   ActionController::RoutingError:
     No route matches [GET] "/home/index"
```

The failure is because we're never planning to have a /home/index route. We're going to use the HomeController#index as the root (or homepage) of our application. We can fix this spec failure by deleting the spec or by changing it to request our root path instead. Let's do the latter:

```
require 'rails_helper'

RSpec.describe 'HomePage', type: :request do
  describe 'GET /index' do
    it 'returns http success' do
      get root_path
      expect(response).to be_successful
    end
end
```

```
    end
  end
```

Our spec should now pass. Our next failure message points to our `spec/requests/pages_spec.rb` spec:

```
1) Pages GET /show returns http success
   Failure/Error: <h2><%= @page.title %></h2>

   ActionView::Template::Error:
     undefined method `title' for nil:NilClass
```

This failure is happening because our `PagesController#show` action is querying our database for a page with a slug value of "show" that does not currently exist. We can fix this by putting a known page instance into our database and then using its slug value in our request spec:

```
require 'rails_helper'

RSpec.describe 'Pages', type: :request do
  describe 'GET /show' do
    let(:page) { create(:page, :published) }

    it 'returns http success' do
      get page_path(slug: page.slug)
      expect(response).to be_successful
    end
  end
end
```

This update gets our spec passing. If we now run RSpec against our entire test suite, we see that we now only have a few warnings:

```
be rspec
```

```
# Not yet implemented
# ./spec/helpers/home_helper_spec.rb:14

# Not yet implemented
# ./spec/helpers/pages_helper_spec.rb:14

# Not yet implemented
# ./spec/views/home/index.html.erb_spec.rb:4
```

```
# Not yet implemented
# ./spec/views/pages/show.html.erb_spec.rb:4
```

We will implement some of these specs in later chapters. For now, let's make our test suite less noisy by just deleting them:

```
rm spec/helpers/home_helper_spec.rb \
   spec/helpers/pages_helper_spec.rb \
   spec/views/home/index.html.erb_spec.rb \
   spec/views/pages/show.html.erb_spec.rb
```

We can now run RSpec against our entire test suite and see that we have no failure messages or warnings.

Summary

We now have a solid understanding of how to create a system spec and how to use Capybara to interact with our application like a user would when using a web browser. We also have a good understanding of how to create custom routes, controller actions, and how to use instance variables in view templates.

Next, we'll jump into view specs, an often overlooked but very important part of our testing suite capabilities.

Build Homepage Contents

8

In the last chapter, we created our first page, the home page, and our show page for displaying individual page objects. These were minimal efforts with just enough content for creating our first two system specs. In this chapter, we will take things further and complete building out these pages using our remaining content fields.

View Specs

If you recall, we used the HTML `<article>` tag to wrap our page content. This is a good choice as it has semantic value for accessibility and search engine optimization. It's not hard to see how our homepage, which uses an `article` tag to list all of our page summaries, will be similar in structure to our `article` tag that shows a single page object on our show page. Hmm.

In fact, the only real difference between the two is that our homepage view will show our page `summary` field, while our show page view will show our `content` field. This similar structure is a good candidate for a shared partial template.

Shared Partial Template

Our shared partial idea needs a spec, so let's create a new file named `_page.html.erb_spec.rb` in our `spec/views/shared` directory and then add the following content:

```
require 'rails_helper'

RSpec.describe 'shared/_page.html.erb', type: :view do
  let(:page) { build(:page) }

  it 'renders the page object' do
    assign(:page, page)
    render partial: 'shared/page',
           locals: {
             page: page,
             content: '<p>content</p>'
```

```
            }
      expect(rendered).to have_css('h2', text: page.title)
      expect(rendered).to have_css('p', text: page.created_at.to_fs)
      expect(rendered).to have_css('p', text: 'content')
   end
 end
```

The filename _page.html.erb_spec.rb may look a little strange, but it's actually a convention for naming view specs for partial templates. The leading underscore indicates that this is a partial template spec, and the _spec.rb suffix is used to indicate that this is a spec file.

The spec itself is fairly straightforward. We build a page object and assign it to a page instance variable, much like our Rails controller would. We use build because we do not need our variable to actually be persisted in our database for the purposes of our spec. We then render our partial template while passing in our *local* variables using locals. Finally, we make assertions about the rendered content.

When we run our new spec, we get the failure message:

```
1) shared/_page.html.erb renders the page object
   Failure/Error:
     render partial: 'shared/page',
              locals: {
                 page: page,
                 content: '<p>content</p>'
              }

   ActionView::MissingTemplate:
     Missing partial shared/_page
```

The failure message makes perfect sense as we have not yet created our partial template. In the app/views/shared directory, let's create an empty _page.html.erb file and then run our spec again. This time, we get a different failure message:

```
1) shared/_page.html.erb renders the page object
   Failure/Error: expect(rendered).to have_css('h2',
   text: page.title)
     expected to find css "h2" but there were no matches
```

This failure is also expected as we have not yet added any content to our partial template. Let's add the following:

```
<article>
  <h2><%= link_to page.title, page_path(slug: page.slug) %></h2>
  <p><%= page.created_at.to_fs %></p>
  <%= content.html_safe %>
</article>
```

This gets our spec passing. We can now refactor our homepage and show page views to use this partial template.

Notably, we use the `html_safe` method on our `content` variable to indicate that it is safe HTML content. This is important as we will likely want to later format our summary and content field data with HTML formatting.

If we were to use the `content` variable without calling `html_safe` on it, our HTML would be rendered as literal text. This is a security feature of Rails to prevent cross-site scripting (XSS) attacks. We can see this undesirable HTML tag rendering in action by temporarily removing the `html_safe` call:

```
<%= content %>
```

Our <p>content</p> tag will now have any dangerous characters replaced with their corresponding HTML entities before being rendered:

```
&lt;p&gt;content&lt;/p&gt;
```

Our < and > characters have been replaced, making our HTML tags safe to render.

So you may now be wondering if using `html_safe` makes our app less secure. We trust ourselves to not attack our own application, so it's likely we can trust that our own content will be safe. If we were to allow untrusted users to create pages, we would not want to use `html_safe` on it before rendering it, or we would put great effort into sanitizing the content before we did render it.

Granted, a <p> tag is not very dangerous, but imagine if we allowed users to create pages with JavaScript <script> tags in them. We would not want to render that JavaScript without sanitizing it as it could be used to attack our site visitors.

More View Specs

We have our shared partial template, but we still need to update our "*homepage*" and "*show*" page views to use it. Let's start with a homepage view spec file named `index.html.erb_spec.rb` in our `spec/views/home` directory:

```
require 'rails_helper'

RSpec.describe 'home/index', type: :view do
  let(:page) { build(:page) }

  it 'renders the page object' do
    assign(:pages, [page])
    render
    expect(rendered).to have_css('h2', text: page.title)
    expect(rendered).to have_css('p', text: page.created_at.to_fs)
    expect(rendered).to include(page.summary)
```

```
    end
  end
```

This spec expects our `home/index` template to use our shared partial template to render a list of page objects, with emphasis on displaying our `summary` field data. We start out with calling `assign` to assign an array of page objects to the `pages` variable just like our controller would, and then we render the view. We can simply call `render` since this is a non-partial template. RSpec knows the correct template to render because of our `RSpec.describe 'home/index' do` block that contains our path. After the render executes, we make assertions about the rendered content.

I will point out how our last expectation uses `include` to check for the presence of our `summary` field data. This is a good choice as we do not want to make any direct assumptions about the actual HTML structure of our summary data. We just want to make sure that the summary data is present in the rendered content.

When we run our spec, we get the failure:

```
1) home/index renders the page object
   Failure/Error: expect(rendered).to have_css('p',
     text: page.created_at.to_fs)
     expected to find css "p" but there were no matches
```

Now we need to update our `home/index` template to use our shared partial:

```erb
<% @pages.each do |page| %>
  <%= render partial: 'shared/page',
             locals: {
               page: page,
               content: page.summary
             } %>
<% end %>
```

Next, let's add our "*show*" view spec file named `show.html.erb_spec.rb` in our `spec/views/pages` directory:

```ruby
require 'rails_helper'

RSpec.describe 'pages/show', type: :view do
  let(:page) { build(:page) }

  it 'renders the page object' do
    assign(:page, page)
    render
    expect(rendered).to have_css('h2', text: page.title)
    expect(rendered).to have_css('p', text: page.created_at.to_fs)
    expect(rendered).to include(page.content)
```

```
    end
  end
```

This spec expects our `pages/show` template to use our shared partial template to render a single page object, just as before, but now with emphasis on displaying our `content` field data, rather than our `summary` data. We start out with calling `assign` to assign our page object to our `page` variable, just like our controller would, and then we render our view. We can again just call `render` since this is also a non-partial template. RSpec again knows the correct template to render because of our `RSpec.describe 'pages/show'` do block that contains the path. After the render, we make assertions about the rendered content.

When we run our spec, we get the failure message:

```
1) pages/show renders the page object
   Failure/Error: expect(rendered).to have_css('p',
     text: page.created_at.to_fs)
     expected to find css "p" but there were no matches
```

Now we need to update our `pages/show` template to use our shared partial:

```
<%= render partial: 'shared/page',
           locals: {
             page: @page,
             content: @page.content
           } %>
```

That's it! We have now refactored our homepage and show page views to use our shared partial template. We have also added view specs to ensure that our partial template is rendering the correct data depending on the context it's used in. Let's re-run all of our specs again to make sure we have not accidentally broken anything:

```
be rspec
```

We should see all of our specs are passing.

Homepage Layout

Until now, we've been using the default Rails application layout file `application.html.erb` located in our `app/views/layouts` directory. It was generated for us when we first created our Rails application. Let's improve on our layout by adding some structure to it. We will go with the familiar `header`, `main`, `sidebar`, and `footer` layout structure shown in Figure 8-1 that many websites use. The `header`, `footer`, and `sidebar` sections will contain more or less static content, while the `main` section will contain the more dynamic content that changes depending on the page we are viewing.

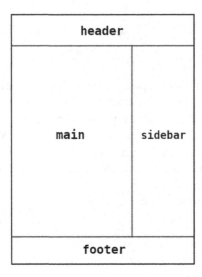

Figure 8-1 Blog page layout

CSS Framework

We will use the CSS framework *Bootstrap* to bootstrap our layout and CSS styling. Bootstrap is a mature CSS framework that is well documented and has many great features. It works really well with mobile devices and has a large community of veteran users. We will use the latest *Bootstrap* version 5.

There are many ways to add *Bootstrap* to a Rails application. Since we are using Rails and have a Gemfile setup already, we will use the gem approach. Let's add the following to our Gemfile in the upper section outside of any environment groups, so it's available to all our environments:

```
gem 'bootstrap'
```

Then we need to run bundle to install the new gem:

```
bundle
```

Layout Template

Right now, our layout <body> tag content looks this:

```
<body>
  <%= render 'shared/header' %>
  <%= yield %>
</body>
```

Currently, we're rendering a shared header partial template and then `yielding` whatever content we get from a given controller action when visiting a particular URL route. Let's add the `main`, `sidebar`, and `footer` sections to our layout and introduce additional partial templates to help keep things organized.

Let's begin this idea with a new view spec. Let's first create a new directory `spec/views/layouts` and then add a new view spec file inside it named `application.html.erb_spec.rb`:

```
require 'rails_helper'

RSpec.describe 'layouts/application', type: :view do
  it 'renders the layout' do
    allow(view).to receive(:render).and_call_original
    render

    expect(view).to have_received(:render).with('shared/header')
    expect(view).to have_received(:render).with('shared/side_bar')
    expect(view).to have_received(:render).with('shared/footer')
  end
end
```

This spec provides a lot of value for the few lines of code it contains. It ensures that our layout is rendering the correct partial templates. The line

```
allow(view).to receive(:render).and_call_original
```

is dual purpose. It allows us to add expectations about `render` calls our view makes, and with the `and_call_original` call, it allows the `render` calls to actually happen even though we are mocking all render calls inside our view. This spec isn't so much about what HTML is rendered, but rather that the correct partial templates are successfully rendered in our layout file.

When we run our spec, we get past the expected `shared/header` rendering since it already exists in our layout file, but then the next expectation fails with the error:

```
Failures:

1) layouts/application renders the layout
   Failure/Error: expect(view).to have_received(:render)
     .with('shared/side_bar')
```

At this point, it makes sense to create empty `shared/side_bar` and `shared/footer` partial templates. Let's do that now. Remember to name the files with leading underscores, `shared/_side_bar.html.erb` and `shared/_footer.html.erb`, respectively, to indicate they are partial templates.

With our new empty partial templates in place, we can update our layout HTML to create our actual layout structure:

```
<body>
  <div class="container-fluid">
    <%= render 'shared/header' %>
  </div>

  <main class="container-fluid">
    <div class="row">
      <div class="col-md-9">
        <%= yield %>
      </div>
      <div class="col-md-3">
        <%= render 'shared/side_bar' %>
      </div>
    </div>
  </main>

  <%= render 'shared/footer' %>
</body>
```

In our layout, we use the Bootstrap `container-fluid` style that will expand our content to fill the entire width of the browser window. Next, we create a `row` and two `col-md-9` and `col-md-3` columns. The `col-md-9` column will contain the `yielded` content from the controller action, while the `col-md-3` column will contain the `side_bar` partial template. We also add a `footer` partial template to the bottom of our layout.

Let's run our view spec again and see that it passes. We can also visit our homepage in a web browser and see that our layout is rendering correctly.

Sidebar Layout

Lots of different types of content can appear in a blog sidebar. Some of the more common things I've seen are

- Recent posts
- Recent comments
- Archives
- Categories
- Tag clouds
- Search
- Social media links

From this list of possible sidebar content, I've chosen to write about two of the most common ones: an archive and a search form. The archive will be a list of all the month/year combinations that have any page content. The search form will allow our visitors to search our pages by title or by content.

Let's capture the layout of our sidebar in a view spec. This new spec will be similar to our application layout spec; it will ensure we are rendering the correct partial templates we mean to render. Let's create a new spec file named _side_bar.html.erb_spec.rb in our spec/views/shared directory with the following content:

```ruby
require 'rails_helper'

RSpec.describe 'shared/_side_bar', type: :view do
  it 'renders the side_bar' do
    allow(view).to receive(:render).and_call_original
    render

    expect(view).to have_received(:render).with('shared/search_form')
    expect(view).to have_received(:render).with('shared/archives')
  end
end
```

Running this spec, we get the following error:

```
Failures:

1) shared/_side_bar renders the side_bar
   Failure/Error: expect(view).to have_received(:render)
     .with('shared/search_form')
```

For now, let's create empty files for our new partial template files:

1. app/views/shared/_search_form.html.erb
2. app/views/shared/_archives.html.erb

Now we can update our shared/_side_bar.html.erb partial template to render our new partials:

```erb
<%= render 'shared/search_form' %>
<%= render 'shared/archives' %>
```

With these changes in place, our side_bar view spec passes.

Summary

In this chapter, we introduced a new layout file and partial templates to help keep our views organized. In the next chapter, we'll build out our search form in earnest, as well as our archive listing.

In the previous chapter, we laid out placeholder templates for our overall application layout and our sidebar. In this chapter, we will build out a search service which will allow us to search our blog pages by keyword. We'll also work up some clever SQL to establish our dynamically generated archive list.

Search As a Service

We'll start this chapter by first building a search *service*. Our search service will be a simple Ruby class that handles searching our page records and will live in between our `Search` controller and our `Page` model. We're going to develop it as a service because it's neither a model nor is it a controller. It will be called from our controller, but it will not *be* a controller, and similarly it will operate on our `Page` model while not *being* a model itself. All that said, it makes sense to develop it as a service.

You may find other Ruby and Rails developers have strong opinions about when to make a thing into a service or not. I've found the best way for me to decide is to ask myself: *Is this thing a model? Is this thing a controller? If neither is true, then it's probably a service.* If you're coming over from the Java world, you may prefer to make a thing into a service even when it could exist just as easily as a *worker* or a *builder/factory* class, or something similar. Feel free to do whatever makes sense to you. I'm going to show you what I do.

I also think it's important to remember that when using Rails, some things we will build won't always fit comfortably into the model-view-controller (MVC) pattern. It's up to us to decide how to handle these things when they come up. Rails doesn't include a formal "*service*" pattern, but it does not mean we are prohibited from making and using services.

Implementing a Search Service

Let's start by creating a new spec directory `spec/services`. This is where we'll put our search service spec. Then, inside our new directory, let's create a new spec file called *page_search_spec.rb*. Inside our new spec file, let's add the following code:

```
require 'rails_helper'
```

```
RSpec.describe PageSearch do
  subject { PageSearch }

  describe '.search' do
    it 'nil params returns no pages' do
      expect(subject.search(nil)).to eq([])
    end
  end
end
```

As expected, we see our new spec fail when we run it:

```
NameError:
  uninitialized constant PageSearch
```

The error message is telling us that we need to create a PageSearch constant of some sort, so let's do that. Let's first create a new directory called app/services. Then, inside our new directory, let's create a new file called page_search.rb. Inside our new file, let's add the following code:

```
module PageSearch
end
```

This will create a new constant as a Ruby Module. But why did we choose a module instead of a class? The reason is that we're not going to be creating any instances of our search service. We're only going to call a single method on it, so it makes sense to make it as a Ruby module. If we were going to be creating actual instances of our search service, then we would have made it a Ruby Class.

When we run our spec again, we see that creating our new module moves us to our next error message:

```
NoMethodError:
  undefined method `search' for PageSearch:Module
```

Spec failures are really good at telling us what we need to do next! Let's add a search method to our PageSearch module:

```
def self.search(params)
end
```

The `self` keyword in Ruby has a number of different meanings depending on the context. In this context, it means that we're defining a method directly inside our `PageSearch` module namespace. This allows us to call it like this:

```
PageSearch.search

# Instead of like this:
# PageSearch.new.search
```

When we run our spec again, we see that creating our new method moves us to our next error message:

```
Failure/Error: expect(subject.search).to eq([])
  expected: []
       got: nil
```

At this point, we can make our spec pass by simply returning an empty array:

```
module PageSearch
  def self.search(params)
    []
  end
end
```

The next thing we will do is get our search service to handle empty parameters. In Ruby, an empty parameter hash is not the same thing as the `nil` value we passed in our first spec. Let's add a new spec to our `page_search_spec.rb` file to capture this idea:

```
it 'empty params returns no pages' do
  expect(subject.search({})).to eq([])
end
```

This spec automatically passes because we're already returning an empty array by default. So now both of our invalid parameter specs are passing.

The next thing we will do is get our search service to handle valid parameters. Before we do that, we need to consider what we will do with the parameters our service receives. Ultimately, we'll use the params to search our database for matching `Page` records, which sounds a lot like a Rails `scope`.

So instead of writing a spec around actual `Page` search results, let's write specs to ensure we send only valid parameters to our `Page` scope:

```
it 'an empty term is not sent to .by_term' do
  allow(Page).to receive(:by_term)
  PageSearch.search({ term: '' })
  expect(Page).to_not have_received(:by_term)
end

it 'a nil term is not sent to .by_term' do
  allow(Page).to receive(:by_term)
  PageSearch.search({ term: nil })
  expect(Page).to_not have_received(:by_term)
end

it 'a valid term is sent to .by_term' do
  allow(Page).to receive(:by_term)
  PageSearch.search({ term: 'foo' })
  expect(Page).to have_received(:by_term).with('foo')
end
```

The `allow` mocks our call to `.by_term`, and our `expect` verifies that our `by_term` call was made or not. The `have_received` matcher verifies that a method was called with the correct arguments. When we run our specs, we see they all fail because we haven't defined the `.by_term` scope yet:

```
Failure/Error: allow(Page).to receive(:by_term)
  ...
  does not implement: by_term
```

We can fix this by stubbing an empty `.by_term` scope, which we will build out shortly, in our `Page` model:

```
scope :by_term, ->(term) { [] }
```

Running our spec again, we see that it fails with a new error message:

```
Failure/Error: expect(Page).to have_received(:by_term).with('foo')
  ...
  expected: 1 time with arguments: ("foo")
  received: 0 times
```

The error message is telling us that we need to call the `.by_term` scope from our `PageSearch` service. But before we do that, we need to consider under what conditions we will call our new

.by_term scope. We only want to call it when we have a term parameter present, so let's implement it that way:

```ruby
def self.search(params)
  return [] unless params.present? && params[:term].present?

  Page.by_term(params[:term])
end
```

We're examining our params in two different ways here. The first way is to check if params are present at all, and if they are not present, we return an empty array, which is similar to searching using Rails ActiveRecord and finding no results. The second way we examine our params is to check if the term key is present, and if so we call our .by_term scope. When we run our specs again, we can see that they now all pass.

Searching by Term

Now that we have our .by_term scope being called from inside our search service, we can start to implement the scope itself. We want to be able to search by any number or combination of terms. So let's start by writing a spec that will allow us to search by a single term. Let's add the following to our existing spec/models/page_spec.rb file:

```ruby
describe '.by_term' do
  let(:page) { create(:page, content: 'foo') }

  before { page }

  it 'returns pages for the given term' do
    expect(Page.by_term('foo')).to eq([page])
  end
end
```

Our spec fails to find an array of Page instances and fails:

```
Failure/Error: expect(Page.by_term('foo')).to eq([page1])
  expected: [#<Page id: 47, user_id: 118, title: "Decipio...>]
       got: []
```

Looks like it's time to implement our stubbed `.by_term` scope. We'll start by assuming that we'll be searching for a single term. This will change later, but right now we're doing TDD, and we're only concerned with this one failing spec. So let's make it pass with

```
scope :by_term, ->(term) { where('content LIKE ?', "%#{term}%") }
```

When we run our spec again, we see that it passes. Now we can move on to implementing the ability to search by multiple terms. Let's add a new spec that will allow us to search by multiple terms:

```
describe '.by_term' do
  let(:page1) { create(:page, content: 'foo') }
  let(:page2) { create(:page, content: 'foo bar') }
  let(:page3) { create(:page, content: 'foo bar baz') }

  before do
    [page1, page2]
  end

  it 'returns pages for the given term' do
    expected = [page1, page2, page3]
    expect(Page.by_term('foo')).to match_array(expected)
  end

  it 'returns pages for multiple terms' do
    expected = [page3]
    expect(Page.by_term('foo baz')).to match_array(expected)
  end
end
```

Our first spec still passes, but our second spec is failing because we're not splitting up the term into individual words. Using the Rails console, we can see that the entire string is being searched for like a phrase using the `.to_sql` method:

```
be rails console

irb(main):001:0> Page.by_term('foo baz').to_sql
=> "SELECT \"pages\".*
   FROM \"pages\"
   WHERE (content LIKE '%foo baz%')"
```

We want to split the phrase into individual words and then use the resulting array to form a dynamically generated SQL query. We also want to take care to not break our existing spec that only queries by one word. We also want to clean up the content of the term or phrase being passed in and only search for alphanumeric characters. Here is the solution I came up with:

```
scope :by_term, ->(term) do
  term.gsub!(/[^-\w ]/, '')
  terms = term.include?(' ') ? term.split : [term]

  pages = Page
  terms.each do |t|
    pages = pages.where('content ILIKE ?', "%#{t}%")
  end

  pages
end
```

There's a lot going on there, so let's break it down. First, we clean up the incoming term argument by removing any non-alphanumeric characters using gsub with the regular expression. The regular expression may look complicated at first glance, but it's really just a list of characters we want to keep in the term while removing all others.

Next, we check to see if the term contains a space character, which indicates that it is a phrase. If it is a phrase, then we split it into individual terms; otherwise, we just put the single term into an array as a single element. This way, we end up with an array either way.

We then iterate over the array of term(s) and build up a query that will search for each term. We start with just assigning Page to pages, then we add on a where clause for each term. Rails will join all of our where clauses together with an SQL AND:

```
irb(main):001:0> Page.by_term('Foo baz!').to_sql
=> "SELECT \"pages\".*
   FROM \"pages\"
   WHERE (content ILIKE '%Foo%')
   AND (content ILIKE '%baz%')"
```

This way, we can search for as many terms as we like, and the query will be built up correctly. If you plan to run this code in production, you might want to limit the array size to some maximum number of terms of course.

Finally, we return the resulting query result. When we run our specs again, we see they are both passing. Now we'll move on to implementing calling our search service from our controller.

Searching for Pages

In the next section, we will add a search form to our sidebar. We will then implement a search controller and view template to display our search results.

Adding a Search Form

Now that we have our search service implemented, we can pursue adding it to our sidebar and begin using it. Since this next bit of functionality is going to involve a form submission, we'll test this using a new system spec. In our `spec/system` directory, we'll create a new file called `search_spec.rb` and add the following code:

```ruby
require 'rails_helper'

RSpec.describe 'Search' do
  describe 'Searching' do
    before do
      create(:page, :published, content: 'Page content')
    end

    context 'with no search term' do
      it 'returns no results' do
        visit root_path

        within 'form' do
          fill_in 'term', with: ''
          click_button 'Search'
        end

        expect(page).to have_current_path(search_path(term: ''))
        expect(page).to have_css('p', text: 'No results found')
      end
    end
  end
end
```

Our spec is fairly straightforward. We create a page with some content, then visit the root path and submit an empty search term. We check that our form is actually set up to perform a GET request when invoked, which will make the URL useful to examine, compared to a form POST. We then expect to see a message saying that no results were found.

There are a lot of missing pieces to get this spec working, and we'll let the spec drive them all out. When we run this spec:

```
be rspec spec/system/search_spec.rb
```

we see that it fails with

```
1) Search Searching with no search term returns no results
   Failure/Error:
     within 'form' do
       fill_in 'term', with: ''
       click_button 'Search'
```

```
      end

    Capybara::ElementNotFound:
      Unable to find css "form"
```

Our failure message tells us that our spec can't find a form on the page. Let's add an actual search form to our `_search_form.html.erb` partial:

```
<div>
  <%= form_for(:search, url: search_path, method: :get) do %>
    <div>
      <input type="search" name="term" />
      <input type="submit" value="Search" />
    </div>
  <% end %>
</div>
```

Now when we run our spec, we get our next failure message:

```
1) Search Searching with no search term returns no results
   Failure/Error: <%= form_for(:search, url: search_path,
     method: :get) do %>

   ActionView::Template::Error:
     undefined local variable or method `search_path' for
       #<ActionView::Base:0x0000000000cbc0>
```

Our spec doesn't currently understand that we're expecting the `search_path` variable to be a Rails route, which makes sense since we didn't add it to our routes file yet. Let's add a new route pointing to our search controller. In our `config/routes.rb` file, let's add

```
get '/search', to: 'search#index'
```

This addition to our routes file will direct a matching GET request to `/search` to an `index` action in our `SearchController`, which of course doesn't exist yet. So as expected, when we run our spec, we get

```
1) Search Searching with no search term returns no results
Failure/Error: raise MissingController.new(error.message, error.name)

ActionController::RoutingError:
  uninitialized constant SearchController
```

The spec is telling us that we need to create a `SearchController`. Let's do that now. In our `app/controllers` directory, let's create a new file called `search_controller.rb` and add the following code:

```ruby
class SearchController < ApplicationController
  def index
  end
end
```

Our new search controller is very simple; it just has an empty `index` action that does nothing useful at the moment. It is the simplest thing we can do to try to move our failing spec along to the next error. When we run our spec again, we're informed of our missing search index template:

```
1) Search Searching with no search term returns no results
Failure/Error: raise ActionController::MissingExactTemplate, message

ActionController::MissingExactTemplate:
  SearchController#index is missing a template for request formats:
    text/html
```

Displaying Search Results

Let's add our missing template. Inside our `app/views` directory, let's add a new directory named `"search"`, and inside that directory, let's create a new file named `index.html.erb`. Running our spec again, we get our next error message:

```
1) Search Searching with no search term returns no results
   Failure/Error:
      expect(page).to have_css('p', text: 'No results found')
         expected to find css "p" but there were no matches
```

Looks like progress. We're now getting a failure because we don't have the *No results found* message on our page. Let's add that to our new template:

```
<p>No results found</p>
```

With that addition, we now have a passing search spec.

Next, we can add a new spec to test the search results display when we do enter an actual search term. In our `spec/system/search_spec.rb` file, let's add the following code:

```ruby
context 'with a search term' do
  it 'renders search results' do
    visit root_path

    within 'form' do
      fill_in 'term', with: 'content'
      click_button 'Search'
    end

    expect(page).to have_current_path(search_path(term: 'content'))

    articles = find_all('article')
    expect(articles.count).to eq(1)

    within articles.first do
      expect(page).to have_css('h2', text: Page.last.title)
    end
  end
end
```

This spec is very similar to our previous spec except this time we're entering an actual search term. We're then expecting to see the title of the page we created previously as the first of an array of `<article>` tags we find using `find_all`. When we run this spec, we get

```
1) Search Searching with a search term renders search results
   Failure/Error: expect(articles.count).to eq(1)
     expected: 1
          got: 0
```

Getting this spec working requires two things. First, we need to get some search results to display. Second, we need to make sure that our search results are actually being rendered inside of `<article>` tags. Let's start with the first problem. In our `SearchController`, we need to add some code to actually perform the search. We'll use our `PageSearch` service to do the search. In our `index` action, let's add

```ruby
class SearchController < ApplicationController
  def index
    @pages = PageSearch.search(params)
  end
end
```

Then, in our associated view template `search/index.html.erb`, we can update our code to iterate over our `@pages` instance variable and render each page inside an `<article>` tag using our `_page.html.erb` partial:

```erb
<% if @pages.any? %>
  <% @pages.each do |page| %>
    <%= render partial: 'shared/page',
               locals: {
                 page: page,
                 content: page.summary
               } %>
  <% end %>
<% else %>
  <p>No results found</p>
<% end %>
```

This gets our failing spec to pass. There's nothing too fancy there; we call any? on our `@pages` variable to check if there are any pages in the collection. The rest is just collection iteration and partial rendering.

If you've been following along closely with the code in this chapter, you'll notice that we just added a block of code that is very similar to a block of code that we added before:

```erb
<% @pages.each do |page| %>
  <%= render partial: 'shared/page',
             locals: {
               page: page,
               content: page.summary
             } %>
<% end %>
```

This same block of code is used in our `home/index.html.erb` file too. We should factor this code out to make our app more DRY (don't repeat yourself). Let's create a new partial called `shared/_pages.html.erb` and move the code from our `home/index.html.erb` action into this new partial. We will leave it mostly the same except we will turn the `@page` instance variable into a local template variable called `Page`:

```erb
<% pages.each do |page| %>
  <%= render partial: 'shared/page',
             locals: {
               page: page,
               content: page.summary
             } %>
<% end %>
```

Now we can use this new partial in both our home/index.html.erb and search/index.html.erb templates. Let's clean things up by updating our home/index.html.erb template to use our new partial:

```
<%= render partial: 'shared/pages', locals: { pages: @pages } %>
```

And then let's update our search/index.html.erb template to do the same:

```
<% if @pages.any? %>
  <%= render partial: 'shared/pages', locals: { pages: @pages } %>
<% else %>
  <p>No results found</p>
<% end %>
```

We performed this refactor to make our app more DRY. We're not repeating ourselves anymore. We're using a partial to render a collection of pages in a single template file instead of repeating the same code in multiple places.

We also performed this refactor "under test," so it was low risk, but we do need to now re-run our specs to make sure they still pass:

```
be rspec spec/system/search_spec.rb spec/system/home_spec.rb
```

It looks like we didn't break anything:

```
...

Finished in 2.51 seconds (files took 1.09 seconds to load)
3 examples, 0 failures
```

Pages Archive

Now that we've got a working search feature for our pages, we can next pursue adding our archived pages feature. We'll add our new *Archives* section below our search form in our sidebar. This section will display a list of month and year links that have pages in them. When a user clicks a month and year link, they will be taken to a page that displays all of the pages that were created in that month and year.

We will tackle this feature in three steps:

1. Create a list of months and years that have pages in them
2. Create a search scope to search pages by month and year
3. Add a link to each month and year combination in our sidebar

Creating a List of Months and Years

We'll start by creating a list of months and years that have pages in them. We can do this by adding a new method to our `Page` model called `.month_year_list`. This method will return an array of hashes that contain `month` and `year` key/value pairs. We'll use these values to create search engine–friendly links in our sidebar. Let's add the following spec to our `page_spec.rb` file:

```
describe '.month_year_list' do
  let(:result) { Page.month_year_list }

  before do
    create(:page, created_at: Date.new(2022, 8, 10))
  end

  it 'returns month and year' do
    expect(result[0]['month_name']).to eq('August')
    expect(result[0]['month_number']).to eq('08')
    expect(result[0]['year']).to eq('2022')
  end
end
```

We will need the `month_number` and `year` values to create our search engine–friendly URLs. We will use the `month_name` and `year` values for the HTML display values of our URLs. The somewhat redundant `month_name` and `month_number` values are personal preference; feel free to use whatever month and year formats you like.

As expected, our spec fails:

```
1) Page.month_year_list returns month and year
   Failure/Error: let(:result) { Page.month_year_list }

   NoMethodError:
     undefined method `month_year_list' for Page:Class
```

Let's add the `.month_year_list` method to our `Page` model:

```
def self.month_year_list
end
```

This progresses our spec failure to the next error:

```
1) Page.month_year_list returns month and year
   Failure/Error: expect(result[0]['month_name']).to eq('August')

   NoMethodError:
     undefined method `[]' for nil:NilClass
```

This error is telling us that our `result` variable is `nil` and that we're trying to access the first element of a nil array. We need to return an array of hashes from our `.month_year_list` method. To extract the month name from our `created_at` timestamp, we can use SQL and some Postgres functions:

```
def self.month_year_list
  sql = <<~SQL
    SELECT
      TO_CHAR(created_at, 'Month') AS month_name
    FROM pages
  SQL
  ActiveRecord::Base.connection.execute(sql)
end
```

This SQL query uses PostgreSQL's `TO_CHAR` function to extract the month name from our `created_at` timestamp field. When we run our spec again, we get a somewhat annoying new error:

```
1) Page.month_year_list returns month and year
   Failure/Error: expect(result[0]['month_name']).to eq('August')

      expected: "August"
           got: "August    "
```

This error is telling us that our `month_name` value has some extra whitespace at the end of it. We can fix this by using the PostgreSQL `TRIM` function:

```
def self.month_year_list
  sql = <<~SQL
    SELECT
      TRIM(TO_CHAR(created_at, 'Month')) AS month_name
    FROM pages
  SQL
  ActiveRecord::Base.connection.execute(sql)
end
```

Now our first expect statement passes, and we get a new error message for our second expect statement:

```
1) Page.month_year_list returns month and year
   Failure/Error: expect(result[0]['month_number']).to eq('08')

      expected: "08"
           got: nil
```

So let's add the `month_number` value to our SQL query:

```ruby
def self.month_year_list
  sql = <<~SQL
    SELECT
      TRIM(TO_CHAR(created_at, 'Month')) AS month_name,
      TO_CHAR(created_at, 'MM') AS month_number
    FROM pages
  SQL
  ActiveRecord::Base.connection.execute(sql)
end
```

When we re-run our spec, we can see this update moves us to the failure for our third expect statement:

```
1) Page.month_year_list returns month and year
   Failure/Error: expect(result[0]['year']).to eq('2022')

      expected: "2022"
           got: nil
```

We can fix this by adding the `year` value to our SQL query:

```ruby
def self.month_year_list
  sql = <<~SQL
    SELECT
      TRIM(TO_CHAR(created_at, 'Month')) AS month_name,
      TO_CHAR(created_at, 'MM') AS month_number,
      TO_CHAR(created_at, 'YYYY') AS year
    FROM pages
  SQL
  ActiveRecord::Base.connection.execute(sql)
end
```

With this addition, our entire spec passes. Next, we need to consider the scenario where we have multiple pages that were created in the same month and year. We don't want to have duplicate month and year values in our list. We can enhance our spec to add a page with the same month and year and then check to see that our list only contains one entry for that month and year:

```ruby
describe '.month_year_list' do
  let(:result) { Page.month_year_list }

  before do
    create(:page, created_at: Date.new(2022, 8, 10))
    create(:page, created_at: Date.new(2022, 8, 11))
  end
```

```
  it 'returns a list of results' do
    expect(result.count).to eq(1)
  end

  it 'returns month and year' do
    expect(result[0]['month_name']).to eq('August')
    expect(result[0]['month_number']).to eq('08')
    expect(result[0]['year']).to eq('2022')
  end
end
```

When we run our spec, we get the exact expected failure:

```
1) Page.month_year_list returns a list of results
    Failure/Error: expect(result.count).to eq(1)

      expected: 1
           got: 2
```

To get our spec passing, we can add a `DISTINCT` modifier to our SQL query. This will modify our results so that we only have one distinct entry for each month and year combination:

```
def self.month_year_list
  sql = <<~SQL
    SELECT DISTINCT
      TRIM(TO_CHAR(created_at, 'Month')) AS month_name,
      TO_CHAR(created_at, 'MM') AS month_number,
      TO_CHAR(created_at, 'YYYY') AS year
    FROM pages
  SQL
  ActiveRecord::Base.connection.execute(sql)
end
```

With this addition, our spec passes. The last thing we need to do is sort our results by year and month. Let's modify our spec, including our previous "returns a list of results" spec, to test this as well:

```
describe '.month_year_list' do
  let(:result) { Page.month_year_list }

  before do
    create(:page, created_at: Date.new(2022, 8, 10))
    create(:page, created_at: Date.new(2022, 8, 11))
    create(:page, created_at: Date.new(2021, 3, 13))
  end
```

```
  it 'returns a list of results' do
    expect(result.count).to eq(2)
  end

  it 'returns month and year' do
    expect(result[0]['month_name']).to eq('August')
    expect(result[0]['month_number']).to eq('08')
    expect(result[0]['year']).to eq('2022')

    expect(result[1]['month_name']).to eq('March')
    expect(result[1]['month_number']).to eq('03')
    expect(result[1]['year']).to eq('2021')
  end
end
```

This adds an earlier month and year combination and some more expect statements to test the ordering of the results.

When we run our spec, we get the expected ordering failure; it's not sorted by year and month yet; instead, we're getting the "natural" ordering based on how the data was stored in our database:

```
1) Page.month_year_list returns month and year
   Failure/Error: expect(result[0]['month_name']).to eq('August')

     expected: "August"
          got: "March"
```

To fix this, we can add an ORDER BY clause to our SQL query:

```
def self.month_year_list
  sql = <<~SQL
    SELECT DISTINCT
      TRIM(TO_CHAR(created_at, 'Month')) AS month_name,
      TO_CHAR(created_at, 'MM') AS month_number,
      TO_CHAR(created_at, 'YYYY') AS year
    FROM pages
    ORDER BY year DESC, month_number DESC
  SQL
  ActiveRecord::Base.connection.execute(sql)
end
```

We order by both the year and month number so that we get the most recent year first and then the most recent month next when we have more than one month in a given year. With this addition, our spec passes.

An archive list entry implies there will be published pages present for that month and year. The last consideration for our `Page.month_year_list` method is that we should filter out any pages that are not yet published. Let's update our spec to include an unpublished page:

```ruby
describe '.month_year_list' do
  let(:result) { Page.month_year_list }

  before do
    create(:page, created_at: Date.new(2022, 7, 4))
    create(:page, :published, created_at: Date.new(2022, 8, 10))
    create(:page, :published, created_at: Date.new(2022, 8, 11))
    create(:page, :published, created_at: Date.new(2021, 3, 13))
  end

  it 'returns a list of results' do
    expect(result.count).to eq(2)
  end

  it 'returns month and year' do
    expect(result[0]['month_name']).to eq('August')
    expect(result[0]['month_number']).to eq('08')
    expect(result[0]['year']).to eq('2022')

    expect(result[1]['month_name']).to eq('March')
    expect(result[1]['month_number']).to eq('03')
    expect(result[1]['year']).to eq('2021')
  end
end
```

When we run our spec, we get the expected failure:

```
1) Page.month_year_list returns a list of results
   Failure/Error: expect(result.count).to eq(2)

     expected: 2
          got: 3
```

To get our spec passing, we can add a WHERE clause to our SQL query to filter out any pages that are not yet published:

```ruby
def self.month_year_list
  sql = <<~SQL
    SELECT DISTINCT
      TRIM(TO_CHAR(created_at, 'Month')) AS month_name,
      TO_CHAR(created_at, 'MM') AS month_number,
      TO_CHAR(created_at, 'YYYY') AS year
    FROM pages
    WHERE published = true
```

```
      ORDER BY year DESC, month_number DESC
   SQL
   ActiveRecord::Base.connection.execute(sql)
end
```

This gets our spec passing.

It's been a fun journey to develop our archive year and month list. It's completely covered with specs, and we have a Ruby method wrapping our SQL query that we can use to get the data we need. We can now use this method to draw our archive list in our view.

Archive List View

In the previous section, we developed a method to get a year/month aggregate list of all the pages in our database. Now we will use this method to draw our archive list in our view and show search results for a given month and year.

Before jumping right into coding our archive list display into our sidebar, we need to consider how it should be wired up. We already have a `PageSearch` service class that handles searching for pages by keyword. We could probably add a new method to this class to handle searching for pages by month and year without too much additional effort. In fact, we already use our `PageSearch` service class in our `SearchController`, so treating archive searching like regular searching seems like a good idea. Let's work toward that goal. A good next step will be to add a spec to our `page_search_spec.rb` to test the searching by month and year:

```
it 'valid year and month are sent to .by_year_month' do
  allow(Page).to receive(:by_year_month)
  PageSearch.search({ year: 2022, month: 8 })
  expect(Page).to have_received(:by_year_month).with(2022, 8)
end
```

When we run our spec, we get the expected failure:

```
1) PageSearch.search valid year and month are sent to .by_year_month
     Failure/Error: allow(Page).to receive(:by_year_month)
       Page(id: integer, user_id: integer ...)
       does not implement: by_year_month
```

We need to add a new method to our `Page` model to handle searching by year and month:

```
scope :by_year_month, ->(year, month) do
  []
end
```

When we run our spec again, we get the expected failure:

```
1) PageSearch.search valid year and month are sent to .by_year_month
     Failure/Error: expect(Page).to have_received(:by_year_month) ...
       Page(id: integer, user_id: integer ...)
           expected: 1 time with arguments: (2022, 8)
           received: 0 times
```

We can fix this failure by improving our parameter handling in our `PageSearch.search` method:

```ruby
def self.search(params)
  return [] unless params.present?

  Page.by_term(params[:term]) if params[:term].present?

  if params[:year].present? && params[:month].present?
    Page.by_year_month(params[:year], params[:month])
  end
end
```

That gets our spec passing. We now know we're sending the correct parameters to our `Page.by_year_month` method. When we have a term parameter, we call our `Page.by_term` method, and when we have year and month parameters, we instead call our `Page.by_year_month` method.

Next, we need to build out our `Page.by_year_month` scope method to actually return the pages for a given year and month. We'll start by adding a spec to our `page_spec.rb` to test the `Page.by_year_month` method:

```ruby
describe '.by_year_month' do
  let(:page1) { create(:page, created_at: Date.new(2022, 8, 10)) }
  let(:page2) { create(:page, created_at: Date.new(2021, 4, 13)) }

  before do
    [page1, page2]
  end

  it 'returns pages for the given year and month' do
    expect(Page.by_year_month(2021, 4)).to match_array([page2])
  end
end
```

When we run our spec, we get the expected failure:

```
1) Page scopes .by_year_month returns pages for the given year ...
   Failure/Error: expect(Page.by_year_month(2021, 4)).to match ...
```

```
    expected collection contained: [#<Page id: 694, user_id: ...
      actual collection contained: []
```

To get this passing, we need to query our database for pages that match the given year and month. We can do this with a parameterized SQL query:

```
scope :by_year_month, ->(year, month) do
  sql = <<~SQL
    extract(year from created_at) = ?
    AND
    extract(month from created_at) = ?
  SQL
  where(sql, year, month)
end
```

Our spec passes with this change. We now have a tested and working `Page.by_year_month` method.

Let's now go back to our `PageSearch.search` method and clean it up a bit. We're passing our incoming params off to the correct scopes, but we're not currently ordering our results nor are we filtering results by our published status. We can easily fix these issues with a few minor changes:

```
def self.search(params)
  return [] unless params.present?

  pages = if params[:year].present? && params[:month].present?
            Page.by_year_month(params[:year], params[:month])
          elsif params[:term].present?
            Page.by_term(params[:term])
          end

  return [] unless pages

  pages.published.ordered
end
```

After that, let's ensure our specs in `page_search_spec.rb` are still passing:

```
be rspec spec/services/page_search_spec.rb
```

And we get the expected results:

```
. . . . . .

Finished in 0.02775 seconds (files took 1.03 seconds to load)
6 examples, 0 failures
```

Archive Integration Testing

With all that, we're now ready to wrap up this chapter with a high-level system spec to test the archive list and search results when we click a month and year link. We'll start by adding a new spec to our spec/system directory called archive_spec.rb:

```ruby
require 'rails_helper'

RSpec.describe 'Archives' do
  describe 'Results page' do
    before do
      create(:page, :published, created_at: '2022-08-10')
    end

    it 'renders archives search results' do
      visit root_path
      click_on 'August 2022'

      articles = find_all('article')
      expect(articles.count).to eq(1)

      within articles.first do
        expect(page).to have_css('h2', text: Page.first.title)
      end
    end
  end
end
```

Next, we'll create a published page with a known creation date which will in turn give us a known archive entry for our sidebar. Then we'll visit our root path and click our known-to-be-present *August 2022* link. We'll then expect to have our one article element on the page.

When we run our spec, we get the expected failure:

```
1) Archives Results page renders archives search results
   Failure/Error: click_on 'August 2022'

   Capybara::ElementNotFound:
     Unable to find link or button "August 2022"
```

This error makes sense since we haven't yet built out our archive sidebar HTML. Let's do that now. Inside our shared/archives partial, let's call our new Page.by_year_month method and iterate over each item to build out our archive HTML links in our sidebar:

```
<div>
  <h4>Archives</h4>
  <ul>
    <% Page.month_year_list.each do |item| %>
      <li>
        <%= link_to
              "#{item['month_name']} #{item['year']}",
              "/search/#{item['year']}/#{item['month_number']}" %>
      </li>
    <% end %>
  </ul>
</div>
```

This will give us a list of links for each month and year that we have pages for, but when we run our spec, we get the following error:

```
1) Archives Results page renders archives search results
   Failure/Error: raise ActionController::RoutingError ...

   ActionController::RoutingError:
     No route matches [GET] "/search/2022/08"
```

Looks like a missing route error. To fix this failure, we need to add a route for our archive link to our config/routes.rb file:

```
get 'search/:year/:month',
    to: 'search#index',
    year: /\d{4}/,
    month: /\d{2}/
```

We use some simple regular expressions to ensure that the year and month are four and two digits, respectively. We do not need to add a controller action for this route since we're already using the `SearchController#index` action for our search results.

When we run our spec again, we see that it passes now.

Summary

In this chapter, we dug into "*Search as a Service*" and built out our search form and our archive list in our sidebar. Our sidebar content will appear on every page and will help our site visitors find the content they're looking for more easily.

We also showed how to make custom Rails routes that will allow us to have beautiful URLs, instead of ugly ones containing query parameters. Search engines prefer these types of URLs, and they're also easier for our users to remember and share.

Page Tags

## 10

In our previous chapter, we built out features for our Page objects. We added a way to search for pages by keyword and a way to look up archives of pages. We did this through a "*search service*," which aided in separating our controller logic from our model logic.

In this chapter, we'll add other features to our pages. We'll add the ability to create and tag pages to categorize them.

Adding Page Tags

First, we want to add the ability to add tags to our Page records. Tags are a way to categorize our pages. Instead of using a gem such as acts-as-taggable-on, we're going to implement our own tagging system. This will give us a better understanding of how tagging systems work and how they can be implemented and customized.

Creating the Tag Model

Let's use a Rails generator to create a Tag model:

```
be rails g model tag \
              name:string:uniq \
              page_tags_count:integer:index
```

This will create several files for us:

```
invoke   active_record
create     db/migrate/20230108193644_create_tags.rb
create     app/models/tag.rb
invoke   rspec
create       spec/models/tag_spec.rb
```

© The Author(s), under exclusive license to APress Media, LLC, part of Springer Nature 2024
G. Donald, *Hands-on Test-Driven Development*,
https://doi.org/10.1007/978-1-4842-9748-3_10

```
invoke        factory_bot
create           spec/factories/tags.rb
```

We're using the `uniq` option to make sure that our tag names are unique; having duplicates serves no purpose. We're also adding a `page_tags_count` column which will allow us to keep track of how many `Page` records are associated with a given tag. We'll use this to determine if a tag can be deleted or not, and it also has the nice side effect of allowing us to sort tags by popularity and not having to count them each time we want to sort them.

Let's run our migrations:

```
be rails db:migrate
be rails db:migrate RAILS_ENV=test
```

Let's first update our `Tag` factory to use a sequence to generate a unique name for each tag:

```
FactoryBot.define do
  factory :tag do
    sequence(:name) { |n| "Name #{n}" }
  end
end
```

Next, let's update our generated `tag_spec.rb` file to add some validation tests:

```
require 'rails_helper'

RSpec.describe Tag, type: :model do
  subject { build(:tag) }

  it { is_expected.to validate_presence_of(:name) }
  it { is_expected.to validate_uniqueness_of(:name) }
end
```

Running our spec, we can see that it fails as expected:

```
1) Tag is expected to validate that :name cannot be empty/falsy
   Failure/Error: it { is_expected.to validate_presence_of(:name) }

   Expected Tag to validate that :name cannot be empty/falsy, but
   this could not be proved.
```

We can fix this failure by adding a :name validation to our Tag model:

```
validates :name, presence: true
```

Running our spec again, we can see that it fails in a new way:

```
1) Tag is expected to validate that :name is case-sensitively unique
   Failure/Error: it { is_expected.to validate_uniqueness_of(:name) }

   Expected Tag to validate that :name is case-sensitively unique,
   but this could not be proved.
```

We can fix this failure by adding a :name uniqueness validation:

```
validates :name, presence: true, uniqueness: true
```

Our Tag spec should now pass.

Creating the Page Tag Model

Next, we need to create a "*join model*" to allow us to associate a Tag to a Page. We'll again use a Rails generator to create this model:

```
be rails g model page_tag \
                 page:references \
                 tag:references
```

Before we run our CreatePageTags migration, we need to update it to add a unique index to our page_id and tag_id columns. This will make sure that we won't ever have any duplicate PageTag records. Let's add this line after the end of our create_table block:

```
add_index :page_tags, %i[page_id tag_id], unique: true
```

With that added, now let's run our migration:

```
be rails db:migrate
be rails db:migrate RAILS_ENV=test
```

Now that we have our `page_tags` table created in our database, let's update our `page_tags` factory to be more useful:

```
FactoryBot.define do
  factory :page_tag do
    page { create(:page) }
    tag { create(:tag) }
  end
end
```

After that, we can next focus on our `page_tag_spec.rb` file. We'll start by adding some validation tests:

```
require 'rails_helper'

RSpec.describe PageTag, type: :model do
  subject { create(:page_tag) }

  it { is_expected.to belong_to(:page) }
  it { is_expected.to belong_to(:tag) }
end
```

Running our spec, we can see that it passes. This is because we generated our `PageTag` model using `:references` for our `Page` and `Tag` columns. This automatically added our `belongs_to` associations for us.

We do need to add an extra bit of code to enable our `page_tags_count` column to be updated automatically when we create or destroy `PageTag` records, but first the spec:

```
it { is_expected.to belong_to(:tag).counter_cache }
```

Then, once we see it fail:

```
Failures:

1) PageTag is expected to belong to tag required: true
   counter_cache => true
   Failure/Error: it { is_expected.to belong_to(:tag).counter_cache }
     Expected PageTag to have a belongs_to association called tag
     (tag should have counter_cache => true)
```

We can fix this failure by adding the `counter_cache` option to our `belongs_to`:

```
belongs_to :tag, counter_cache: true
```

Let's now prevent our database from raising an error if we try to create a duplicate `PageTag` record. We can do this by adding a validation spec:

```
it { is_expected
  .to validate_uniqueness_of(:tag_id)
  .scoped_to(:page_id) }
```

This one actually fails as we might have expected:

```
1) PageTag is expected to validate that :tag_id is case-sensitively
   unique within the scope of :page_id
     Failure/Error: is_expected.to validate_uniqueness_of(:tag_id)
                      .scoped_to(:page_id)

   Expected PageTag to validate that :tag_id is case-sensitively
   unique within the scope of :page_id, but this could not be proved.
```

We can fix this by adding a validation to our `PageTag` model:

```
validates :tag_id, uniqueness: { scope: :page_id }
```

That should do it for our `PageTag` model. It's a pretty simple model, but it's important to get it right as it's the glue model that will allow us to associate `Tag` records to `Page` records.

Jumping Over Relationships

One of the most useful features in Rails is the ability to jump over relationships using a `has_many :through` association. This association allows us to create a `has_many` relationship on a model and then use that relationship to create another `has_many` relationship on a related model. In our case, we want to be able to jump from an instance of a `Page` to its related `Tags`, or from a `Tag` to its related `Pages`.

In other words, we want to be able to do things like this:

```
Page.last.tags.each do |tag|
  puts tag.name
end
```

or this:

```
Tag.last.pages.each do |page|
  puts page.title
end
```

We basically want to be able to ignore our `PageTag` join model. Let's add some new specs to our `page_spec.rb` file to test this behavior:

```
it { is_expected.to have_many(:page_tags).dependent(:destroy) }
it { is_expected.to have_many(:tags).through(:page_tags) }
```

Running our specs, we can see that they both fail:

```
1) Page is expected to have many page_tags dependent => destroy
   Failure/Error: it { is_expected.to have_many(:page_tags) ...
     Expected Page to have a has_many association called page_tags
     (no association called page_tags)

2) Page is expected to have many tags through page_tags
   Failure/Error: it { is_expected.to have_many(:tags) ...
     Expected Page to have a has_many association called tags
     (no association called tags)
```

Getting these specs to pass is simple. We just need to add our `has_many` associations to our `Page` model:

```
has_many :page_tags, dependent: :destroy
has_many :tags, through: :page_tags
```

Now we can add similar specs to our `tag_spec.rb` file:

```
it { is_expected.to have_many(:page_tags).dependent(:destroy) }
it { is_expected.to have_many(:pages).through(:page_tags) }
```

Running our specs, we can see that they both fail:

```
1) Tag is expected to have many page_tags dependent => destroy
   Failure/Error: it { is_expected.to have_many(:page_tags) ...
     Expected Tag to have a has_many association called page_tags
```

```
      (no association called page_tags)

2) Tag is expected to have many pages through page_tags
   Failure/Error: it { is_expected.to have_many(:pages) ...
     Expected Tag to have a has_many association called pages
     (no association called pages)
```

Again, getting these sorts of specs to pass is easy. We just need to add our has_many associations to our Tag model:

```
has_many :page_tags, dependent: :destroy
has_many :pages, through: :page_tags
```

We can now very easily jump across our relationships and ignore our PageTag join model.

Tagging Pages

Now that we have our PageTag model and our has_many :through associations neatly defined and tested, we can start working on our tagging feature itself. We want to be able to pass a comma-separated list of Tag names to our Page model and have it create the appropriate PageTag records for us. We need it to handle the case where a Tag already exists, as well as the case where it does not.

After Save Callbacks

We'll call our new comma-separated list of Tag names a "*tags_string*." We can process it when we save an instance of a Page. Let's capture this idea by adding a new spec to our page_spec.rb file:

```ruby
describe '#update_tags' do
  let(:page) { create(:page, tags_string: 'foo, bar') }

  context 'when tags do not already exist' do
    it 'creates new tags' do
      expect { page }.to change(Tag, :count).by(2)
      expect(page.tags.map(&:name)).to match_array(%w[foo bar])
    end
  end
end
```

Running our new spec, we can see that it fails:

```
1) Page#update_tags when tags do not already exist creates new tags
   Failure: let(:page) { create(:page, tags_string: 'foo, bar') }

   NoMethodError:
     undefined method `tags_string=' for #<Page id: nil, user_id: ...
```

The failure message is telling us that we need to add a `tags_string` attribute to our `Page` model. We can do that by adding the following to our `Page` model:

```
attr_accessor :tags_string
```

An `attr_accessor` is a special type of Ruby method that allows us to read and write to a named instance variable. In our case, we're creating a new instance variable named `tags_string` that we can use to store a comma-separated list of `Tag` names, each of which we want to assign to our `Page` object. We don't actually want to store our `tags_string` value in our database, but we do need it to be accessible inside our `Page` model for a period of time. We can use an `attr_accessor` to do exactly that.

This change moves us on to our next failure message:

```
1) Page#update_tags when tags do not already exist creates new tags
   Failure/Error: expect { page }.to change(Tag, :count).by(2)
     expected `Tag.count` to have changed by 2, but was changed by 0
```

We need to add a way for our `Page` model to handle the updating of new `Tag` records after we save an instance of a `Page` object. We can do that by using a Rails `after_save` callback:

```ruby
after_save :update_tags

private

def update_tags
  return if tags_string.blank?

  tags_string.split(',').each do |name|
    name = name
            .downcase
            .gsub(/[_ ]/, '-')
            .gsub(/[^-a-z0-9+]/, '')
            .gsub(/-{2,}/, '-')
            .gsub(/^-/, '')
            .chomp('-')

    tags << Tag.find_or_create_by(name:)
```

```
    end
  end
```

Every time we save a `Page` instance, our `update_tags` method will be called. It will return early if our `tags_string` is blank; otherwise, it will split our `tags_string` into an array of *names* and then iterate over the array. For each name, we clean it up, just like how we previously cleaned up our `title` field to make our `slug` field. We then find or create a new `Tag` record with that name. Finally, we find or create a `PageTag` record, connecting our `Page` to that `Tag`.

But what about the case where we remove a `Tag` from our `tags_string`? We need to also remove the corresponding `PageTag` record. We need to add a spec to our `page_spec.rb` file to make sure we always remove any tags not in our `tags_string` when our callback is called. Inside our existing "#update_tags" describe block, let's add the following:

```ruby
context 'when tags are removed' do
  let(:tag_names) { page.tags.map(&:name) }

  before { page }

  it 'removes tags' do
    page.update(tags_string: 'foo')
    expect(tag_names).to match_array(%w[foo])
  end
end
```

We add a `before` block to our spec to make sure we have a persisted `Page` instance with the two known `Tag` records from our previous spec. Then we update our `Page` object with a new `tags_string` and expect one of the tags to be removed. Running this spec, we can see that it fails:

```
1) Page#update_tags when tags are removed removes tags
   Failure/Error: expect(tag_names).to match_array(%w[foo])

      expected collection contained:  ["foo"]
      actual collection contained:    ["bar", "foo"]
      the extra elements were:        ["bar"]
```

To get this passing, we need to clear out all of our `PageTag` records via our `has_many :tags` association before we create new ones. Let's update our `update_tags` method to do that:

```ruby
def update_tags
  self.tags = []
  return if tags_string.blank?

  tags_string.split(',').each do |name|
    name = name
```

```
            .downcase
            .gsub(/[_ ]/, '-')
            .gsub(/[^-a-z0-9+]/, '')
            .gsub(/-{2,}/, '-')
            .gsub(/^-/, '')
            .chomp('-')

      tags << Tag.find_or_create_by(name:)
   end
 end
```

Admittedly, adding `self.tags = []` is a quick and dirty solution. In the future, when our blog is massively popular and we have written millions of `PageTag` records into our database, and we need to optimize this code, we can cherry-pick exactly the records that we want to destroy by iterating through them and then only destroying those. But for now, this will work just fine.

Display Tags on Pages

Now that we can create `Tag` records when we save a `Page`, we want to display them as `Tag` name links. When we click a link, we want to see a list of all the `Page` records that are associated with that particular `Tag`. So the first thing to do is to create a helper method to display our `Tag` records as links. Let's make a helper spec to capture this idea. In our `spec/helpers` directory, let's create a new `tags_helper_spec.rb` file with the following contents:

```
require 'rails_helper'

RSpec.describe TagsHelper, type: :helper do
  describe '#tag_links' do
    let(:page) { create(:page, tags_string: 'foo, bar') }
    let(:result) { helper.tag_links(page.tags) }

    it 'returns a list of tag links' do
      expected = <<~HTML.squish
        <a href="/tags/bar">bar (1)</a>
        <a href="/tags/foo">foo (1)</a>
      HTML
      expect(result).to eq(expected)
    end
  end
end
```

This spec will drive out a lot of the functionality we want. We'll pass in a `Tag` collection and get back a list of links. We'll also want to see the number of `Page` records associated with each `Tag`, and we'll want to see the `Tag` names in alphabetical order.

Let's run our spec and see what happens:

```
NameError:
  uninitialized constant TagsHelper
```

This is telling us that we need to create our `TagsHelper` module. So let's do that. In our `app/helpers` directory, let's create a new file called `tags_helper.rb` with the following contents:

```
module TagsHelper
end
```

Now let's run our spec again:

```
NoMethodError:
undefined method `tag_links'

  let(:result) { helper.tag_links(page.tags) }
```

Our next failure message is telling us that we need to add our `tag_links` method to our `TagsHelper` module. Let's do that:

```
module TagsHelper
  def tag_links(tags)
  end
end
```

Now let's run our spec again:

```
Failure/Error: expect(result).to eq(expected)

expected: "<a href=\"/tags/bar\">bar (1)</a> <a ... "
     got: nil
```

We're getting closer. Our spec is now failing because we're not returning the correct value, our new tag links. Let's fix that:

```
module TagsHelper
  def tag_links(tags)
    tags.map do |tag|
```

```
        link_to "#{tag.name} (#{tag.page_tags_count})",
                tag_path(tag.name)
    end.join(' ')
  end
end
```

We iterate over our `tags` array and create a link for each one. Now our spec failure message is telling us that we have not yet defined a `tag_path` route:

```
NoMethodError:
  undefined method `tag_path'
```

Let's add our new route to our `config/routes.rb` file:

```
get 'tags/:name', to: 'tags#show', name: /[-a-z0-9_+]*/, as: :tag
```

Now let's run our spec again:

```
1) TagsHelper#tag_links returns a list of tag links
   Failure/Error: expect(result).to eq(expected)

     expected: "<a href=\"/tags/bar\">bar (1)</a> <a ...
          got: "<a href=\"/tags/foo\">foo (1)</a> <a ...
```

We're now getting links, but they are in the wrong order. We want them to be in alphabetical order. This is easy; we can add a scope to our `Tag` model to sort by name:

```
scope :ordered, -> { order(:name) }
```

Then we update our spec to use this new scope:

```
let(:result) { helper.tag_links(page.tags.ordered) }
```

This gets our spec to pass.

I will pause here to mention that we could have made the choice to use a `default_scope`. Some software engineers (myself included) consider it to be potentially dangerous as it can be difficult to override and can lead to unexpected behavior when doing complex table joins.

We can now proceed with using our new `TagsHelper#tag_links` method in our views. We'll start by adding a new system spec to capture this usage. In our `spec/system` directory, we'll create a new `tag_spec.rb` file with the following contents:

```ruby
require 'rails_helper'

RSpec.describe 'Tag', type: :system do
  let(:page_1) { create(:page, :published, tags_string: 'foo, bar') }
  let(:page_2) { create(:page, :published, tags_string: 'bar') }

  before do
    [page_1, page_2]
  end

  it 'displays clickable tags on a page' do
    visit root_path

    find_link(href: '/tags/foo').click
    expect(page).to have_content(page_1.title)
    expect(page).to_not have_content(page_2.title)

    find_link(href: '/tags/bar', match: :first).click
    expect(page).to have_content(page_1.title)
    expect(page).to have_content(page_2.title)
  end
end
```

When we run this spec, we'll see that it fails:

```
1) Tag displays clickable tags on a page
   Failure/Error: find_link(href: '/tags/foo').click

   Capybara::ElementNotFound:
     Unable to find link nil with href "/tags/foo"
```

We need to add a call to our new `tag_links` method in our `_page.html.erb` partial that will cause our tag links to appear at the bottom of each page or page summary. Let's add that:

```erb
<p><%= tag_links(page.tags).html_safe %></p>
```

Running our spec again, we can see a new failure message:

```
ActionController::RoutingError:
  uninitialized constant TagsController
```

We could use a Rails generator here to create our missing `TagsController`, but it's not a lot of effort to step through it manually. Let's create our new `tags_controller.rb` file in our `app/controllers` directory:

```
class TagsController < ApplicationController
end
```

Running our spec again, we can see a new failure message:

```
AbstractController::ActionNotFound:
  The action 'show' could not be found for TagsController
```

Let's do as the error message suggests and create a `show` action in our `tags_controller.rb` file:

```
class TagsController < ApplicationController
  def show
  end
end
```

Running our spec again, we can see a new failure message:

```
ActionController::MissingExactTemplate:
  TagsController#show is missing a template for request formats:
  text/html
```

Again, letting the failure message guide us, let's create the directory `app/views/tags` and then create a new `show.html.erb` file inside it.

Once we've done that, we can run our spec again and see the next failure message:

```
1) Tag displays clickable tags on a page
    Failure/Error: expect(page).to have_content(page_1.title)
      expected to find text "Page Title ..."
```

This failure message occurs after we visit our `root_path` and click a tag. We can see that the `show` action is being called, but we're not seeing any pages. This is because we haven't yet implemented the logic to find the pages that have the tag we clicked. Let's do that by adding the following to our show action in our `tags_controller.rb` file:

```ruby
def show
  tag = Tag.find_by(name: params[:name])
  @pages = tag.pages.published.ordered
end
```

We also need to actually render our @pages in our show.html.erb file. We can do that by adding the following to our show.html.erb file, reusing our _pages.html.erb partial:

```erb
<%= render partial: 'shared/pages', locals: { pages: @pages } %>
```

With those changes in place, we can run our spec again and see that it passes.

Handling Missing Tags

We've now implemented the ability to click a tag and see the pages that have that tag. But what happens if we try to visit a tag that doesn't exist? Let's add a spec to capture this behavior. In the same system spec we've been working in, `tag_spec.rb`, we'll add the following new spec:

```ruby
context 'when a tag does not exist' do
  it 'redirects to the root path' do
    visit '/tags/does-not-exist'
    expect(page).to have_current_path(root_path)
  end
end
```

Honestly, this spec could just as easily exist as a request spec, but we're going to keep it in our system spec for now since we already have a very similar tag spec. When we run this spec, we'll see that it fails with the following error:

```
1) Tag when a tag does not exist redirects to the root path
   Failure/Error: @pages = tag.pages.published.ordered

   NoMethodError:
     undefined method `pages' for nil:NilClass
```

We need to handle the case where the tag is not found. Let's do that by adding a redirect to our root_path in our show action:

```ruby
def show
  tag = Tag.find_by(name: params[:name])
  redirect_to root_path and return unless tag

  @pages = tag.pages.published.ordered
end
```

With that change in place, we can run our spec again and see that it passes. We redirect and return early to prevent the rest of the show action from being executed, if a tag is not found.

Refactor Duplicate Code

We've made a lot of progress with page tagging, but along the way we've created some duplication in our code. Let's clean that up. We currently have two places in our code where we are cleaning up a string using the same duplicated cleanup code:

```ruby
.downcase
  .gsub(/[_ ]/, '-')
  .gsub(/[^-a-z0-9+]/, '')
  .gsub(/-{2,}/, '-')
  .gsub(/^-/, '')
  .chomp('-')
```

Let's refactor this into a separate Ruby module and remove the duplication. In our spec/models directory, we'll create a new name_cleanup_spec.rb file with the following contents:

```ruby
require 'rails_helper'

RSpec.describe NameCleanup do
  let(:name) { ' - -Foo Bar! _ 87 -- ' }

  describe '.clean' do
    it 'cleans a name' do
      expect(NameCleanup.clean(name)).to eq('foo-bar-87')
    end
  end
end
```

Running our new spec gives us an expected failure message:

```
NameError:
  uninitialized constant NameCleanup
```

Let's create our `NameCleanup` module. In our `app/models` directory, let's create a new file named `name_cleanup.rb` with the following contents:

```ruby
module NameCleanup
end
```

This addition moves us to the next failure:

```
1) NameCleanup.clean cleans a name
   Failure/Error: expect(NameCleanup.clean(name)).to eq('foo-bar-87')

   NoMethodError:
     undefined method `clean' for NameCleanup:Class
```

We can fix this by adding our `clean` method to our `NameCleanup` module and using our cleanup code in it:

```ruby
module NameCleanup
  def self.clean(name)
    name
      .downcase
      .gsub(/[_ ]/, '-')
      .gsub(/[^-a-z0-9+]/, '')
      .gsub(/-{2,}/, '-')
      .gsub(/^-/, '')
      .chomp('-')
  end
end
```

This gets our spec to pass.

Now we can go back to our `Page` model and use our new `NameCleanup` module to clean up our `make_slug` method:

```ruby
def make_slug
  return unless title

  self.slug = NameCleanup.clean(title)
end
```

and then also our `update_tags` method:

```
def update_tags
  self.tags = []
  return if tags_string.blank?

  tags_string.split(',').each do |name|
    name = NameCleanup.clean(name)

    tags << Tag.find_or_create_by(name:)
  end
end
```

Another option to refactor this code might have been to create a local private method instead of our `NameCleanup` module. But testing it as a private method would have required us to test it through each of its callers, with lots of additional test setup, or by calling it indirectly using Ruby's `send` method. I think the module approach is a much better option in this case.

After this refactor, our `Page` model is looking much better. Let's be sure to re-run our `page_spec.rb` spec to make sure we didn't break anything.

Summary

In this chapter, we've added the ability to tag pages and view pages by tag. We also refactored some of our code to remove duplication. In our next chapter, we'll begin pursuing our image storage feature.

Images

11

In this chapter, we will add the ability to store image files for display in our blog posts. We will leverage the Active Storage gem to provide much of the functionality while working within our own image controller to serve up the image data and to handle missing images.

Active Storage for Images

Rails version 5.2 introduced a new feature called *Active Storage* that provides file storage functionality. Active Storage allows us to upload files to our Rails application, storing the file binary data as well as metadata, making it the current best way to add images to our blog. I say *"current best way"* because there are many other ways to add images to our blog, but Active Storage is the easiest and most integrated way to do it, given we're already using Rails.

Getting Started with Active Storage

Active Storage will need us to create three new tables in our database:

1. active_storage_blobs
2. active_storage_variant_records
3. active_storage_attachments

Fortunately, we don't need to know much about them with Rails having a generator command to create our database migrations for us:

```
be rails active_storage:install
```

© The Author(s), under exclusive license to APress Media, LLC, part of Springer Nature 2024
G. Donald, *Hands-on Test-Driven Development*,
https://doi.org/10.1007/978-1-4842-9748-3_11

Let's run that command and then migrate our database:

```
be rails db:migrate
be rails db:migrate RAILS_ENV=test
```

Next, we need to inform Active Storage how we would like to store our files. We can do this by adding two configurations to our `config/storage.yml` file, one for our test environment and one for our development environment:

```
test:
  service: Disk
  root: <%= Rails.root.join("tmp/storage") %>

local:
  service: Disk
  root: <%= Rails.root.join("storage") %>
```

It's likely these configurations will already exist in your own Rails application code, but please do check to make sure.

We will cover adding a production environment configuration for storage in a later chapter. For now, we'll just need to configure our development and test environments, and we'll use the `Disk` service for both.

Two more storage configurations that may also already exist in your own Rails application code are in the `config/environments` directory, the `development.rb` and the `test.rb` files.

Inside of `development.rb`, we need to ensure the following line is present:

```
config.active_storage.service = :local
```

And inside of `test.rb`, we need to similarly ensure a similar line exists:

```
config.active_storage.service = :test
```

The point of these two lines is to tell Active Storage which service, from the services defined in our `storage.yml`, to use for each environment.

That's all we need to do to configure our Active Storage setup for local development and test usage.

Adding an Image Model

To actually begin to use Active Storage, we need to create a Rails ActiveRecord model that will represent our image record. This model will be simple, having only a name field. We'll then use Active Storage to attach image data to this model.

Let's create our model with the following command:

```
be rails g model Image name:string
```

Then we'll migrate our database:

```
be rails db:migrate
be rails db:migrate RAILS_ENV=test
```

We want to make sure instances of our Image always have a name present, so let's add a validation spec to our `spec/models/image_spec.rb` file:

```
describe 'validations' do
  it { should validate_presence_of(:name) }
end
```

This spec will fail because we haven't added the validation to our Image model yet:

```
1) Image validations is expected to validate that :name cannot be
   empty/falsy
   Failure/Error: it { should validate_presence_of(:name) }

      Expected Image to validate that :name cannot be empty/falsy,
      but this could not be proved.
```

Let's add the validation to our model:

```
validates :name, presence: true
```

This spec should now pass. Next, let's make sure we have a valid Image factory to use in future specs we will write. Let's add the following to our `spec/models/image_spec.rb` file:

```
describe 'has a valid factory' do
  it { expect(build(:image)).to be_valid }
end
```

The point of this sort of test is to ensure our Image factory, with no traits applied, is always working. I consider this a good habit to get into since RSpec's subject does this implicitly, as well as other factory associations.

Running our spec, we can see that it passes. Now let's update our `Image` factory to give it a name and attach image data:

```
FactoryBot.define do
  factory :image do
    name { 'Name' }

    after(:build) do |image|
      io = Rails.root.join('spec/factories/images/image.jpeg').open
      image.image.attach(io: io,
                          filename: 'image.jpeg',
                          content_type: 'image/jpeg')
    end
  end
end
```

The code `image.image.attach` means that we want our image model to have an `image` field that we can attach data to. The `io` variable is a file handle to a file named `image.jpeg`.

Running our spec again, we can see that it now fails:

```
1) Image has a valid factory
   Failure/Error: io = Rails.root.join('spec/factories/images/ ...

   Errno::ENOENT:
     No such file or directory @ rb_sysopen - ... image.jpeg
```

This error message informs us that we need to provide an `image.jpeg` file. Let's create a directory for our image files:

```
mkdir spec/factories/images
```

And then I'll leave it up to you to find an image file to use for this spec. Any old jpeg file will work; just be sure to name it "*image.jpeg*" and place it in the `spec/factories/images` directory that we just created.

Assuming you've successfully provided an image file, we can now run our spec again, and it will fail with a different error:

```
1) Image has a valid factory
   Failure/Error:
     image.image.attach(io: io,
                        filename: 'image.jpeg',
                        content_type: 'image/jpeg')

   NoMethodError:
```

```
undefined method `image' for #<Image id: nil, name: "Name",
created_at: nil, updated_at: nil>
```

Now we can add the Active Storage attachment code to our model. We'll do this by adding the following to our `app/models/image.rb` file:

```
has_one_attached :image
```

`has_one_attached` is an Active Storage helper method that will provide instances of our model with an `:image` field to which we can attach image data. We could of course call our `:image` field something else if we wanted to, perhaps `:photo`, but we'll stick with `:image`.

Running our spec again, we can see that it now passes.

We could add more validations to our `Image` model, but for now we'll leave it as is. In particular, you might question why we do not have a validation for `image` data being present. For this, we're trusting in the Active Storage gem to do the right thing and to have adequate test coverage in place within its own codebase.

Serving Images

We have our images stored in our database, and so we now need a way to serve them up to our site visitors. We'll do this by creating a controller that will serve up image data from Active Storage.

Adding an Image Controller

A blog wouldn't be complete without the ability to display images in the page content here and there. So we'll need an `ImagesController` with a `show` action to serve up image data.

As you might expect, we'll first write a spec for it, a request spec to be exact. Inside our `spec/requests` directory, let's add a new file called `images_spec.rb` and add the following to it:

```
require 'rails_helper'

RSpec.describe 'Images' do
  it 'returns an image' do
    create(:image)
    get image_path(Image.last)

    expect(response).to be_successful
    expect(response.content_type).to eq('image/jpeg')
  end
end
```

In this spec, we create an `image` record using our new image factory and then make a GET request to our `show` action in our `ImagesController`. We then assert that the response is successful and

that the content type is image/jpeg. This spec will fail in various ways as we work through the
implementation of our controller action. Let's see what the first failure message looks like:

```
be rspec spec/requests/images_spec.rb
```

RSpec tells us that we have an undefined method, a Rails route to be specific:

```
1) Images returns an image
   Failure/Error: get image_path(Image.last)

   NoMethodError:
     undefined method `image_path' ...
```

So let's add a route to our config/routes.rb file:

```
resources :images, only: :show
```

We're adding a standard REST "resources" route, but we only want to make the show action
available. We can see what that gives us by running the rails routes command with the -g
(grep) option to filter the output:

```
be rails routes -g images
```

We can see that Rails has created just the one show route for us:

```
Prefix Verb URI Pattern              Controller#Action
 image GET  /images/:id(.:format)  images#show
```

Running our spec again, we can see that we now have a different error:

```
1) Images returns an image
   Failure/Error: get image_path(Image.last)

   ActionController::RoutingError:
     uninitialized constant ImagesController
```

Looks like it's time to create our image controller. We could use the following command to create it, but we won't because it will create a bunch of extra files that we don't need:

```
# be rails g controller images show
```

Instead, let's create the controller file manually. Let's add a new file to our `app/controllers` directory called `images_controller.rb` and then add the following to it:

```
class ImagesController < ApplicationController
end
```

Running our spec again, we can see that we now have a different error:

```
1) Images returns an image
   Failure/Error: get image_path(Image.last)

   AbstractController::ActionNotFound:
     The action 'show' could not be found for ImagesController
```

RSpec is telling us that it's now time to create a `show` action in our controller. Let's do that:

```
class ImagesController < ApplicationController
  def show
  end
end
```

Running our spec again, we see that we now have a different error:

```
1) Images returns an image
   Failure/Error: get image_path(Image.last)

   ActionController::MissingExactTemplate:
     ImagesController#show is missing a template for request
     formats: text/html
```

Rails wants us to add an HTML/ERB template for use with our `show` action, but what it doesn't currently know is that we're not going to render HTML; we're instead going to serve up binary image data. Once we have our controller action implemented, Rails will no longer complain about

the missing template. Let's add the following code to our show action, and then we will run through
how it works:

```
def show
  img = Image.find_by(id: params[:id])
  image = img.image

  data = image.download
  type = image.content_type
  ext = image.filename.to_s.split('.').last
  filename = "image_#{img.id}.#{ext}"

  send_data data, type:, filename:, disposition: 'inline'
end
```

First, we get our img record from our database using the id parameter from our request params. We
then get the Active Storage image attachment from the img record. Next, we assign our variables
data, type, and filename for use with the Rails send_data method to return the image data
to our controller action's caller.

The real magic here is the image.download call. This is an Active Storage method that will
download the image data from wherever it is stored, locally or remotely. It returns the downloaded
binary image data to us, and we then pass that data to the Rails send_data method.

The filename is not required, but it's a nice touch to give the image a friendly name that is
probably more uniform than the original filename of the image that was uploaded. We're also setting
the disposition to inline so that the image will be displayed in the browser, rather than be
automatically downloaded.

Let's run our spec again and see that it passes.

There are other things we could do in our request spec, such as checking the headers, to make sure
the Content-Disposition is set to inline, for example:

```
headers = response.headers
expect(headers['Content-Disposition']).to include('inline')

image_name = "image_#{Image.last.id}.jpeg"
expect(headers['Content-Disposition']).to include(image_name)
```

Or we could check for and handle a missing image file extension in the filename; it's up to you
whether you want to add these to your own specs or not.

We do however want to handle the situation where the "img" record is not found. It may have been
deleted from our database, or the id parameter may have been incorrectly set by the caller. Let's add
a spec for handling that scenario:

```
it 'returns a missing image if the image does not exist' do
  get image_path(0)

  expect(response).to be_successful
```

```
    expect(response.content_type).to eq('image/jpeg')
  end
```

Instead of showing a broken image, we want to show a "missing" image. We can simulate that scenario by looking for an image with an id of 0. We can then check that the response is successful and the content type is image/jpeg, just like if the image was actually found.

Running our spec, we can see that it fails:

```
1) Images returns a missing image if the image does not exist
   Failure/Error: image = img.image

   NoMethodError:
     undefined method `image' for nil:NilClass
```

We can now update our controller action code to handle our missing image scenario:

```
def show
  img = Image.find_by(id: params[:id])

  if img
    image = img.image

    data = image.download
    type = image.content_type
    ext = image.filename.to_s.split('.').last
    filename = "image_#{img.id}.#{ext}"
  else
    image_path = Rails.public_path.join('missing.jpeg')
    image = image_path.open('rb')

    data = image.read
    type = 'image/jpeg'
    filename = 'missing.jpeg'
  end

  send_data data, type:, filename:, disposition: 'inline'
end
```

Running this spec again, we can see that it's still failing, but for a different reason:

```
1) Images returns a missing image if the image does not exist
   Failure/Error: image = image_path.open('rb')

   Errno::ENOENT:
     No such file or directory @ rb_sysopen - ... missing.jpeg
```

Let's add a `missing.jpeg` file to our `public` directory. I will again leave it up to you to provide whatever image you like for your missing.jpeg image file. Let's re-run our spec and see that it now passes.

Summary

In this chapter, we added the ability to upload images and retrieve them using Active Storage. We've also added the ability to handle missing images. We'll add the ability to delete images in a later chapter, when we build out our admin pages. Next, we're going to tackle user authentication.

User Authentication

12

Eventually, our blog application will have an administration interface, and we will need to make sure that only an administrator user can access it. To this end, we will need to add the ability to authenticate to our user model. This chapter will cover how to do that.

Some readers may begin wondering why we are not using a third-party authentication library such as Devise. The reasons are

- We want to always keep our application as simple as possible, with as few dependencies as possible. As you will soon see, adding a user model with salted password authentication is not difficult.
- It's important for software engineers to understand at least the basics of how third-party libraries such as Devise work, so we can make informed decisions to use them or not, and to adequately assess risk when we do choose to use them. Can you trust the authors to ship security fixes quickly when exploits become publicly known?
- We are curious software engineers and want to thoroughly understand how to implement and test basic authentication.

Improving Our User Model

We created a `User` model in a previous chapter. We now need to add functionality to support authentication. In particular, we need to add a password "salt" field and a password "hash" field. Adding these two fields will enable us to store one-way hashed passwords, individually salted for each of our users.

Password Hashing

Password hashing is a technique that is used to safely store passwords in a database in a way that makes it difficult to recover the original password. The idea is that the password is hashed using a one-way hash function, such as SHA-256. The hash function is a mathematical function that takes a string of characters and produces a different fixed length string of characters representing the original

© The Author(s), under exclusive license to APress Media, LLC, part of Springer Nature 2024   133
G. Donald, *Hands-on Test-Driven Development*,
https://doi.org/10.1007/978-1-4842-9748-3_12

value. The hash function is one-way in that it is easy to compute the hash of a string of characters, but it is difficult to compute the original string of characters from the hash. The hash function is also deterministic, in that given the same string of characters the hash function will always produce the same hashed value.

The hash function combines a "*salt*" value with the user-provided password value to produce a password hash. The salt value is a random string of characters, but it is unique for each password. The salt value is stored in the database along with the password hash. The salt value is used to make it difficult to precompute a table of password hashes. If the salt value was not used, an attacker could precompute a table of password hashes for a large number of common passwords and then compare the password hashes in our database to the precomputed table to determine the passwords. Using salt values makes this attack much more difficult, especially for users who use weak passwords.

Now that we have a basic understanding of password salting and hashing, let's add our password fields to our user model.

Adding Fields to Our User Model

Let's generate a migration to add our password fields to our user model:

```
be rails g migration add_user_password_fields
```

We will add two new fields to our user model, a `password_salt` field and a `password_hash` field. Both fields will be strings. Let's modify our new migration file to add the fields:

```
class AddUserPasswordFields < ActiveRecord::Migration
  def change
    add_column :users, :password_salt, :string
    add_column :users, :password_hash, :string
  end
end
```

Now let's run the migration:

```
be rails db:migrate
be rails db:migrate RAILS_ENV=test
```

We now have the fields we need to store password hashes in our `User` model. The next step is to add the ability to set a password for a user. We do not want to store the password in our database in plaintext, so we need to be able to control things explicitly. We need a temporary password field that we can use to generate the value we will actually store in our database.

Inside our `spec/models/user_spec.rb` file, let's capture this idea by adding the following new spec:

```
describe 'set a password' do
  let(:user) { build(:user) }

  it 'sets a password' do
    user.password = 'changeme'
    user.save!

    expect(user.password_salt).to be_present
    expect(user.password_hash).to be_present
  end
end
```

This spec fails because we have not yet added any sort of `password` attribute or method to our user model:

```
1) User password= sets a password
   Failure/Error: user.password = 'changeme'

   NoMethodError:
     undefined method `password=' for #<User id: nil, name: ...
```

The failure message indicates that we don't actually need an attribute; we instead need a `password=` method.

```
def password=(password)
  self.password_salt = 'salt'
  self.password_hash = "#{password_salt}#{password}"
end
```

This gets our spec to pass, but it is not a very good implementation. We're capturing the basic idea of salting a password, but nothing is actually being hashed. We can see what is actually happening by running our Rails console:

```
be rails c
```

When we create a new user, we can see that the password salt and password hash are being set, but not hashed:

```
irb(main):001:0> user = User.new(
  email: 'foo@bar.com',
  name: 'Name',
  password: 'changeme'
)
...
irb(main):002:0> user.password_salt
=> "salt"
irb(main):003:0> user.password_hash
=> "saltchangeme"
```

Being software engineers, but probably not expert cryptographers, we need to add a hashing library to our application.

Add a Hashing Library

We will use the bcrypt gem to add password hashing to our application. The bcrypt gem is a Ruby wrapper around the OpenBSD bcrypt library. Let's add the gem to our application:

```
bundle add bcrypt
```

Next, we need to require the bcrypt library in our User model:

```
require 'bcrypt'
```

This will give us access to all of the bcrypt gem's functionality. We can now modify our password= method to use bcrypt:

```
def password=(password)
  self.password_salt = BCrypt::Engine.generate_salt
  self.password_hash = BCrypt::Engine.hash_secret(
    password,
    password_salt
  )
end
```

First, we generate a salt value using BCrypt::Engine.generate_salt. Then we use the salt value to generate a hash of the user-provided password string using BCrypt::Engine.hash_secret. The salt and hash values are then stored in our user record, after our before_save callback is executed.

Let's re-run our spec and see that it still passes. And then let's see what we're actually storing in our database, now that we're using `bcrypt`:

```
be rails c
```

```
irb(main):001:0> User.destroy_all
...
irb(main):002:0> user = User.new(
  email: 'foo@bar.com',
  name: 'Name',
  password: 'changeme'
)
...
irb(main):003:0> user.password_salt
=> "$2a$12$jOaFNA79pCgwWS0poghAlu"
irb(main):004:0> user.password_hash
=> "$2a$12$jOaFNA79pCgwWS0poghAluIaInS7I98yvVEdi03apOaXSoE5b1uyy"
```

Our salt and password hashes are being stored in our database now. Next, we should perform some actual user validation to verify that our new hash values are being generated correctly and that we can successfully authenticate.

Authenticating a User

Let's add a new spec to verify that we can authenticate a user:

```
describe '.authenticate' do
  let(:user) { build(:user) }
  let(:password) { 'changeme' }

  before do
    user.password = password
    user.save!
  end

  it 'can authenticate' do
    expect(User.authenticate(user.email, password)).to eq(user)
  end
end
```

The idea here is that a user can authenticate if they provide the correct email address and password. We will call an `.authenticate` class method to verify the user's credentials against the values we have stored in our database.

Running this spec, we will see it fail because we have not yet added our .authenticate class method to our User model:

```
1) User.authenticate can authenticate
   Failure/Error: expect(User.authenticate(user.email, password)).to
   eq(user)

   NoMethodError:
     undefined method `authenticate' for User:Class
```

If we implement the .authenticate method:

```
def self.authenticate
end
```

we can make some progress to our next failure message:

```
1) User.authenticate can authenticate
   Failure/Error:
     def self.authenticate
     end

   ArgumentError:
     wrong number of arguments (given 2, expected 0)
```

RSpec is telling us that we need to accept two arguments into our .authenticate method: the user's email address and the password they are attempting to authenticate with. Let's add those arguments:

```
def self.authenticate(email, password)
end
```

Now that we have a method that accepts two arguments, we get our next failure message:

```
1) User.authenticate can authenticate
   Failure/Error: expect(User.authenticate(user.email, password)).to
   eq(user)

     expected: #<User id: 40, name: "First10 Last10", email: ...
          got: nil
```

We're accepting the correct arguments, but we're not actually doing anything with them. Let's add some code to find the user record by email address and then verify that the provided password matches our stored password hash:

```ruby
def self.authenticate(email, password)
  user = User.find_by(email: email)

  password_hash = BCrypt::Engine.hash_secret(
    password,
    user.password_salt
  )

  if password_hash == user.password_hash
    user
  end
end
```

We're again using one-way hashing to generate a hash of the user-provided password and our stored salt value. If our generated hash matches our stored hash, we know that the correct password has been provided, and so we return the user record. If the hashes do not match, we will reach the end of our method, and our return value would be nil since nothing was actually returned.

Our spec should now pass, and this is a good start to our authentication, but we're not done yet. There are a few more things we should do to improve our implementation; we should

1. Return nil if the user's email address is unknown.
2. Handle email address case sensitivity.
3. Create wrapper methods for any BCrypt methods we're using.

Improving Authentication

Right now, we're assuming a user record will always be found when searching by email address, and then we go on to call `User.password_salt` and `User.password_hash`. Either of these two calls will raise an exception if the user record is nil. We should not assume a user will be found and instead return nil if the user's email address is unknown in our database. Let's add a spec to reproduce the issue:

```ruby
it 'unknown email fails authentication' do
  expect(User.authenticate('foo@bar.com', password)).to be_nil
end
```

When we run this spec, we get the following error:

```
1) User.authenticate unknown email fails authenticate
   Failure/Error: user.password_salt
```

```
NoMethodError:
    undefined method `password_salt' for nil:NilClass
```

Let's fix this by returning nil early in our method if the user record is not found:

```ruby
def self.authenticate(email, password)
  user = User.find_by(email: email)
  return nil if user.nil?

  password_hash = BCrypt::Engine.hash_secret(
    password,
    user.password_salt
  )

  if password_hash == user.password_hash
    user
  end
end
```

The next issue we have is that we're not handling email address case sensitivity correctly. If a user signs up with an email address of foo@bar.com and then attempts to authenticate with an email address of Foo@Bar.com, we should still authenticate them. The easiest solution to this is to downcase the email address when we store it in our database and then downcase the email address again when we search for it in our find_by call. This way, we will only ever compare lowercased email addresses. Let's add a spec to handle downcasing email addresses anytime we save a user record:

```ruby
describe 'email' do
  context 'on create' do
    let(:user) { create(:user, email: 'Foo@baR.Com') }

    it 'is downcased' do
      expect(user.email).to eq('foo@bar.com')
    end
  end

  context 'on update' do
    let(:user) { create(:user, email: 'foo@bar.com') }

    before do
      user.update(email: 'Foo@baR.Com')
    end

    it 'is downcased' do
      expect(user.email).to eq('foo@bar.com')
    end
```

```
    end
  end
```

When we run this spec, we get two failures:

```
1) User email on create is downcased
   Failure/Error: expect(user.email).to eq('foo@bar.com')

     expected: "foo@bar.com"
          got: "Foo@baR.Com"

2) User email on update is downcased
   Failure/Error: expect(user.email).to eq('foo@bar.com')

     expected: "foo@bar.com"
          got: "Foo@baR.Com"
```

Let's fix these spec failures by adding a `before_save` callback into our `User` model:

```
before_save :downcase_email

private

def downcase_email
  self.email = email.downcase
end
```

These changes will ensure that anytime we save a user record, on create or on update, our user's email address will be downcased. Our two new specs should pass now, and we can return to improving our authentication method.

Inside our `.authenticate` method, we're not handling email address case sensitivity yet. Let's add a spec to reproduce this issue:

```
it 'mixed case email can authenticate' do
  expect(User.authenticate(user.email.titleize, password)).to eq(user)
end
```

We can use `titleize` as a simple way to uppercase the first letter of the email address. This fails as expected:

```
1) User.authenticate mixed case email can authenticate
   Failure/Error: expect(User.authenticate(user.email.titleize,
   password)).to eq(user)
```

```
    expected: #<User id: 80, name: "First12 Last12", email: ...
         got: nil
```

To fix this, we need to downcase the email address before we search for the user record:

```
def self.authenticate(email, password)
  user = User.find_by(email: email.downcase)
  ...
end
```

Re-running our spec, we see that it now passes, but we just created a new issue. What if the email address is nil? We'll get an exception when we try to call downcase on a nil value. Let's add a spec to reproduce this issue:

```
it 'nil email fails authentication' do
  expect(User.authenticate(nil, password)).to be_nil
end
```

This spec fails as expected:

```
1) User.authenticate nil email fails authentication
   Failure/Error: user = User.find_by(email: email.downcase)

   NoMethodError:
     undefined method `downcase' for nil:NilClass
```

We can fix this by adding a guard clause to our method to return nil early if the email address is nil:

```
def self.authenticate(email, password)
  return nil unless email.present?

  user = User.find_by(email: email.downcase)
  ...
end
```

Re-running our spec, we see that it now passes.

Next, let's do some refactoring. We're using the BCrypt gem to create our password salt and hash values, but what if in the future we decided to use a different gem or even a different algorithm? We would have to change our code in multiple places. Let's extract the logic for creating a password hash into a separate method:

```
def self.hash_password(password, salt)
  BCrypt::Engine.hash_secret(password, salt)
end
```

We can then use this method in our `password=` method:

```
def password=(password)
  self.password_salt = BCrypt::Engine.generate_salt
  self.password_hash = User.hash_password(password, password_salt)
end
```

and also in our `.authenticate` method:

```
def self.authenticate(email, password)
  return nil unless email.present?

  user = User.find_by(email: email.downcase)
  return nil if user.nil?

  password_hash = hash_password(
    password,
    user.password_salt
  )

  if password_hash == user.password_hash
    user
  end
end
```

Let's also create a wrapper method for `BCrypt::Engine.generate_salt`:

```
def self.generate_salt
  BCrypt::Engine.generate_salt
end
```

We can then use this method in our `password=` method:

```
def password=(password)
  self.password_salt = User.generate_salt
  self.password_hash = User.hash_password(password, password_salt)
end
```

We're still depending on the BCrypt gem, but we've isolated the code that depends on it so that if we decide to change gems or algorithms in the future we only have to change the code in one place, and our specs will likely continue to pass.

Always remember to re-run specs to make sure nothing regressed into a broken state when refactoring code or when adding wrapper methods to isolate third-party APIs, as we just did.

Password Confirmation

Since our user password value is one-way hashed, it would be a good idea to confirm it before saving it. We will never be able to look into our database to confirm it after the save occurs, so we need to confirm it before the save.

Let's add new shoulda-matcher specs to capture this confirmation behavior:

```
it { is_expected.to validate_presence_of(:password) }
it { is_expected.to validate_confirmation_of(:password) }
```

Our first failing spec is for the presence of the password:

```
1) User validations is expected to validate that :password cannot be
   empty/falsy
   Failure/Error: it { is_expected.to validate_presence_of(:password)
   }

   NoMethodError:
     undefined method `password' for #<User id: nil, name: ...
```

We don't have an actual password attribute on our user model, and we don't want one either. We only want to store the password hash and salt, never the plaintext version a user provides. So to fix this, we need to add a virtual attribute to our user model:

```
attr_accessor :password
```

And we need to set it inside our password= method:

```
def password=(password)
  @password = password
  self.password_salt = User.generate_salt
  self.password_hash = User.hash_password(password, password_salt)
end
```

These changes will move us to our next failure message:

```
1) User validations is expected to validate that :password cannot be
   empty/falsy
   Failure/Error: it { is_expected.to validate_presence_of(:password)
   }

      Expected User to validate that :password cannot be empty/falsy,
      but this could not be proved.
        After setting :password to <nil>, the matcher expected the
        User to be invalid, but it was valid instead.
```

It appears our new password attribute is correctly defined now, but we need to actually validate it for presence. We can do this by adding a validation to our user model:

```
validates :password, presence: true
```

This change gets our new spec to pass but breaks many of our other specs. The problem is the `subject` defined at the top of our `User_spec.rb` file:

```
subject { build(:user) }
```

If we look at our user factory definition in `spec/factories/users.rb`, we can see that it does not currently define a password attribute, which is an easy fix:

```
password { 'changeme' }
```

Re-running our spec file shows us progress. We're now getting a new failure message for our password confirmation spec:

```
1) User validations is expected to validate that
   :password_confirmation matches :password
   Failure/Error: it { is_expected.to
     validate_confirmation_of(:password) }

   Shoulda::Matchers::ActiveModel::AllowValueMatcher::Attribute ...
     The matcher attempted to set :password_confirmation on the User
     to "some value", but that attribute does not exist.
```

To fix this, we need to update our user password validation to include confirmation:

```
validates :password, presence: true, confirmation: true
```

This change will enable another virtual attribute in our user model, `password_confirmation`, which is exactly what our spec is looking for. This causes us to also need to add a separate password confirmation validation:

```
validates :password_confirmation, presence: true
```

As before, this gets our new spec to pass but breaks some of our other specs. Our `subject` is again causing problems, and we again need to update our user factory definition, this time to include a password confirmation attribute:

```
password_confirmation { password }
```

We'll let FactoryBot reuse the `password` attribute we defined earlier to set our new `password_confirmation` attribute. This will make it easier to change both values in the future if we need to.

This gets our spec to pass, but do we always want to require a password and password confirmation?

Skipping Password Validation

Right now, we are requiring a password and a password confirmation for every user record, both on create and on save. This is not always what we want. For example, if we're only updating a user's name, we don't want to require the password and password confirmation to also be present. We can even imagine a scenario where the user is not even present when another field needs to be updated.

First, let's prove the problem actually exists with a spec, and then we'll figure out how to fix it:

```
describe 'password' do
  before { subject.save! }

  it 'is not required when updating name' do
    user = User.last
    expect(user.password).to be_nil

    user.update(name: 'New Name')
    expect(user).to be_valid
  end
end
```

Running this spec, we can see that the bug is real:

```
1) User password is not required when updating name
   Failure/Error: expect(subject).to be_valid
     expected #<User id: 462, name: "New Name", email:
     "user16@example.com", created_at:
     "2023-01-22 21:10:55.920524000 +0000", updated_at:
     "2023-01-22 21:10:55.920524000 +0000", password_salt:
     [FILTERED], password_hash: [FILTERED]> to be valid, but got
     errors: Password can't be blank, Password confirmation can't
     be blank
```

We can fix this by making our password validations conditional. There are two conditions where we do want the password validation:

1. When the user has not been saved to our database
2. When the user is updating their password

We can first create a private helper method to check for these conditions:

```ruby
private

def password_required?
  !persisted? || password.present?
end
```

So if the user record has not been persisted to our database, because the record is new, or the password is actually present, because the user is updating their password, then we want to execute our password and password confirmation validations. We just need to update our validations to use this helper method to allow them to become conditional:

```ruby
validates :password,
          presence: true,
          confirmation: true,
          if: :password_required?

validates :password_confirmation,
          presence: true,
          if: :password_required?
```

This change gets our new spec to pass.

Summary

In this chapter, we learned how to add a password authentication system to our User model. We learned how to use the bcrypt gem to hash and salt our passwords. We also learned how to use the shoulda-matchers gem to validate password and password confirmation values. We also provided specs and fixes around the password validations to ensure that we only require passwords when we should.

No Devises were harmed in the making of this chapter.

Administration

13

In this chapter, we will develop an administrative interface for our blog's application data. Everything we've built so far will be given the usual CRUD operations (Create, Read, Update, Delete) we'd expect to have available. We will save a lot of time by leveraging Active Admin to create these interfaces.

Adding Active Admin

Active Admin is a gem that provides a framework for creating administrative interfaces for Rails applications. It is a very powerful tool that can be implemented simply and quickly, but can also be customized to a great degree.

Adding the Gem

The first step is to add the gem to our project:

```
bundle add activeadmin
```

Next, we need to run the generator to install the necessary integration files:

```
be rails generate active_admin:install --skip-users --skip-comments
```

We will skip the user integration and instead use our own User model for our user authentication. We will also skip the additional Active Admin comments table as we will not be using admin comments in our blog application.

© The Author(s), under exclusive license to APress Media, LLC, part of Springer Nature 2024   149
G. Donald, *Hands-on Test-Driven Development*,
https://doi.org/10.1007/978-1-4842-9748-3_13

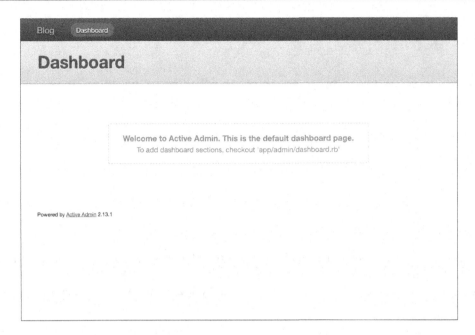

Figure 13-1   Active Admin dashboard

That's it for the setup. We can now start using Active Admin to create our administrative interfaces. Let's start up Rails:

```
be rails s
```

And see what we have so far. Visiting the admin URL shows us output like Figure 13-1:

http://localhost:3000/admin

It's not much at the moment, but we will build it out soon enough.

Testing Active Admin

Active Admin is recipe driven. We will use a DSL (domain-specific language) provided by Active Admin to tell it what we want it to do for us. As a rule, I don't usually write specs for third-party gems that already have their own specs, but Active Admin is a special case. Our Active Admin interface code can be considered part of our application and should be tested as such. Our DSL code could very well contain bugs or could become broken by future changes in our models, for example, so we will write high-level system specs to protect us from our future selves.

Logging In

The first thing we should pursue is to prevent anonymous access to our admin interface. Right now, we can access it without logging in; it's completely unprotected. Let's begin with a system spec to test that we can't access the admin interface without logging in. In our `spec/system` directory, let's create a new file called `login_spec.rb` and add the following code:

```
require 'rails_helper'

RSpec.describe 'Login Page' do
  let(:user) { create(:user) }

  it 'Admin requires logging in' do
    visit admin_root_path

    expect(page).to have_css('h2', text: 'Sign in')

    fill_in 'Email', with: user.email
    fill_in 'Password', with: 'changeme'
    click_button 'Submit'

    expect(page).to have_css('h2', text: 'Dashboard')

    click_link 'Logout'

    expect(page).to have_link 'My Blog'
  end
end
```

In our spec, we try, as an anonymous user, to visit our admin dashboard page and then expect to be redirected away to our login page where we should be encouraged to log in. We then fill in our login form, submit it, and expect to be redirected to our admin dashboard. Finally, we click the logout link and expect to be redirected back to our blog's public homepage. It's a very simple spec, but it will go a long way in helping us drive out our admin login/logout implementation code.

When we run this spec, we see it fails with the following error:

```
1) Login Page Admin requires logging in
   Failure/Error: expect(page).to have_css('h2', text: 'Sign in')
     expected to find visible css "h2" with text "Sign in" but there
     were no matches.
```

To get past this particular error, we need to make several changes:

1. Implement our login form
2. Add a Rails route to render our login form
3. Have Active Admin redirect anonymous users

For the first item, we will need to create a new view template to render our login form. In our app/views directory, let's create a new directory called sessions and inside that directory create a new file called new.html.erb with the following content:

```
<%= form_for(:login, url: login_path) do |f| %>
  <h2>Sign in</h2>
  <div>
    <%= f.label :email %>
    <%= f.email_field :email %>
  </div>
  <div>
    <%= f.label :password %>
    <%= f.password_field :password %>
  </div>
  <div>
    <button type="submit">Submit</button>
  </div>
<% end %>
```

Next, we need to add our new route to our config/routes.rb file:

```
get 'login', to: 'sessions#new'
```

Instead of using the Rails resources method, we will use the get method to create a named route called login that maps to a controller named sessions with a method of new. This will enable the Rails login_path helper method for us.

Next, we need to enable user authentication in Active Admin. In our config/initializers/active_admin.rb file, we need to uncomment the following line:

```
config.authentication_method = :authenticate_admin_user!
```

If you read the comment above this line:

```
# This setting changes the method which Active Admin calls (within
# the application controller) to return the currently logged in user.
```

We know from reading the comment that we need to create a new method in our application_controller.rb file called authenticate_admin_user! that will be called by Active

Admin to authenticate our users. We can verify this is the next thing to pursue by running our spec again:

```
1)  Login Page Admin requires logging in
    Failure/Error: send(active_admin_namespace.authentication_method)
    if active_admin_namespace.authentication_method

    NoMethodError:
      undefined method `authenticate_admin_user!' for
      #<Admin::DashboardController:0x0000000000f4d8>
```

Let's add the following method to our `application_controller.rb` file:

```ruby
def authenticate_admin_user!
  redirect_to login_path if session[:admin_user_id].nil?

  @current_admin_user = User.find_by(id: session[:admin_user_id])
end
```

This method will redirect anonymous users to our login page. We consider a user to be anonymous if they do have a session variable name `admin_user_id` set. If they do have the session variable we're looking for, then we query our database to try to locate their user account. Either way, we set the query result (nil or other) to an instance variable name `@current_admin_user`.

We can now run our spec again and see that we're getting a new failure message:

```
1)  ActionController::RoutingError:
      uninitialized constant SessionsController
```

This error is telling us that we need to create our `sessions` controller. Let's do that now by creating a new file called `sessions_controller.rb` in our `app/controllers` directory and adding the following code:

```ruby
class SessionsController < ApplicationController
end
```

Running our spec again, we see that we've moved along to the next error message:

```
1)  Login Page Admin requires logging in
    Failure/Error: <%= form_for(:login, url: login_path) ...

    ActionView::Template::Error:
      undefined local variable or method `sessions_path'
```

Why is it not complaining about our lack of a new method in our sessions controller? Well, as it turns out, Rails will look for a view template with the same name as the controller method, and if it finds one, it will automatically render it. In our case, we do have a view template called new.html.erb in our app/view/sessions directory, so Rails will render that for us.

So what does the error message mean?

By default, our form_for helper method is creating an HTML form tag for us that contains a method of post and an action of sessions_path. That particular Rails route does not currently exist in our application, so we need to add it. Let's do that now by adding the following line to our config/routes.rb file:

```
post 'login', to: 'sessions#create'
```

This will give us a second login route that maps to a create method in our sessions controller. We can verify this by running the Rails routes command:

```
be rails routes -g login
```

The output shows both new login routes, one for get and one for post:

```
Prefix Verb URI Pattern       Controller#Action
 login GET  /login(.:format)  sessions#new
       POST /login(.:format)  sessions#create
```

Running our spec again, we see that we've moved along to the next error message:

```
AbstractController::ActionNotFound:
  The action 'create' could not be found for SessionsController
```

In order to fix this error, we need to add our create method to our sessions controller. Let's do that now by adding the following code to our sessions_controller.rb file:

```
class SessionsController < ApplicationController
  def create
  end
end
```

Running our spec again, we see that we've moved along to the next error message:

```
1) Login Page Admin requires logging in
   Failure/Error: expect(page).to have_css('h2', text: 'Dashboard')
     expected to find css "h2" but there were no matches
```

This error is telling us that we're submitting our login form successfully, but after that we're not redirecting to the dashboard page. It's time to implement the contents of our `create` method in our `SessionsController`:

```ruby
def create
  user = User.find_by(email: params[:login][:email])
  if User.authenticate(user&.email, params[:login][:password])
    session[:admin_user_id] = user.id
    redirect_to admin_root_path
  else
    render :new
  end
end
```

Our `params` hash will contain a top-level `login` key that contains another hash with our actual login form data. We can query our database using the `email` key of this inner hash to try to locate a matching user account. We then try to authenticate the user using our `User.authenticate` method we added to our `User` model earlier, making sure to use the `&.` safety operator to avoid a nil error if the user account is not found. If the user is authenticated, we set the session variable `admin_user_id` and redirect to our admin dashboard page. If the user is not authenticated, we render the `new` view template again.

Running our spec again, we see that we've moved along to the next error message:

```
1) Login Page Admin requires logging in
   Failure/Error: click_link 'Logout'

   Capybara::ElementNotFound:
     Unable to find link "Logout"
```

It looks like our login is finally working. Now we need to work on our logout functionality.

There are several steps we will work through to get our logout link working:

1. Add a Rails route for our logout link
2. Add a `destroy` method in our `sessions` controller
3. Configure Active Admin to show our logout link

Let's start by adding a Rails route for our logout link. We'll add the following line to our `config/routes.rb` file:

```
get 'logout', to: 'sessions#destroy'
```

Again, we're using a named route. This gives us a `logout` path that maps to a `destroy` method in our `sessions` controller. We can verify this by running the Rails `routes` command:

```
be rails routes -g logout
```

It gives us the following output confirming our new route:

```
Prefix Verb URI Pattern        Controller#Action
logout GET   /logout(.:format) sessions#destroy
```

We could have just as easily used a `delete` route instead of a `get` route if we wanted to. A `delete` route would be more RESTful, but we're not actually making any sort of destructive changes to our database, so we'll use a `get` route instead.

Next, we need to add our `destroy` method in our `SessionsController`. Let's do that now by adding the following code:

```
def destroy
  session[:admin_user_id] = nil
  redirect_to root_path
end
```

This method simply clears the `admin_user_id` session variable and redirects us to our homepage. Without the session variable, any future requests to our admin dashboard will be redirected to our login page.

Finally, we need to configure Active Admin to actually show our logout link; it's off by default. We need to uncomment and/or (re)configure the following variables in our `active_admin.rb` initializer file:

```
config.current_user_method = :current_admin_user
config.logout_link_path = :logout_path
config.logout_link_method = :get
```

The `logout_link_path` and the `logout_link_method` need to match our previous work in our routes and sessions controller. We point them to our `logout_path` that uses the `get` method.

The `current_user_method` variable tells Active Admin which method to call on our `ApplicationController` to get the current user via our login session variable. We still need to add that, so let's add this method to our `ApplicationController`:

```
def current_admin_user
  @current_admin_user ||= User.find_by(id: session[:admin_user_id])
end
```

We memoize the result of our `User.find_by` database query so that we don't query our database every time we call this method. Active Admin can and will call this method multiple times during a single HTTP request, so our ||= memoization adds some efficiency.

Running our spec again, we can see it's finally passing. We've successfully implemented our login and logout functionality for our admin.

Admin Layout

Right now, our login page is using our default `application.html.erb` layout file, so it includes our header and sidebar sections. It would be nice to have a separate layout file for our login page that does not include anything extra. In addition, it could also be laid out and styled differently. We can accomplish this by creating a new layout file and assigning it in our `SessionController`.

Let's first add an expectation to make sure we're rendering the correct layout file. We don't really need an entire new spec for testing that one layout or another is being used, and we can easily look for the presence of a specific element on the page to make sure we're using the one we mean to. Let's add the following expectation just inside the beginning of our "Admin requires logging in" spec in our `login_spec.rb` system spec file:

```
expect(page).to have_css('h2', text: 'Admin')
```

This expectation will look for an h2 element with the text `Admin` just before we try to log in. This will fail because we're not currently using the correct layout file:

```
1) Login Page Admin requires logging in
   Failure/Error: expect(page).to have_css('h2', text: 'Admin')
     expected to find css "h2" but there were no matches
```

Let's fix that now by creating a new layout file called `admin.html.erb` in our `app/views/layouts` directory. We'll add the following content to our new layout file:

```
<!DOCTYPE html>
<html>
  <head>
    <title>Admin</title>
```

```
      <%= csrf_meta_tags %>
      <%= csp_meta_tag %>
      <%= stylesheet_link_tag "application", "data-turbo-track": "reload" %>
    </head>
    <body>
      <h2>Admin</h2>
      <%= yield %>
    </body>
</html>
```

Next, we need to inform our `SessionsController` that it should use our new layout file. We can do that by adding the following line to our `SessionsController` class near the top:

```
class SessionsController < ApplicationController
  layout 'admin'

  ...
end
```

This gets our spec passing. We're now using the correct layout file for our login page.

Managing Pages

Now that we have our Active Admin login and logout functionality working, we can begin adding data management interfaces. We'll first add `Pages`. Inside of our `spec/system` directory, we'll create a new directory called `admin`, then inside of that new directory, we'll create a new file called `pages_spec.rb` with the following content:

```
require 'rails_helper'

RSpec.describe 'Pages' do
  let(:user) { create(:user) }

  describe 'A new page' do
    it 'can be added' do
      visit admin_root_path

      fill_in 'Email', with: user.email
      fill_in 'Password', with: 'changeme'
      click_button 'Submit'

      expect(page).to have_css('h2', text: 'Dashboard')

      visit new_admin_page_path

      select User.last.name, from: 'User'
```

```
        fill_in 'Title', with: 'Page Title'
        fill_in 'Summary', with: 'Summary info'
        fill_in 'Content', with: 'Content goes here'
        fill_in 'Tags', with: 'foo, bar'

        check('Published')

        click_button 'Create Page'

        within '.flashes' do
          expected = 'Page was successfully created.'
          expect(page).to have_css('.flash_notice', text: expected)
        end

        within '#main_content' do
          expect(page).to have_css('td', text: user.name)
          expect(page).to have_css('td', text: 'Page Title')
          expect(page).to have_css('td', text: 'Summary info')
          expect(page).to have_css('td', text: 'Content goes here')
          expect(page).to have_css('span.yes', text: 'YES')
          expect(page).to have_css('td', text: 'bar, foo')
        end
      end
    end
  end
end
```

This spec is a bit more complicated than our previous system specs. We're going to log in, then we're going to create a new page with some basic form field values. We'll then verify that the page was created by checking the HTML that is styled with the flashes CSS class and the HTML with the main_content id attribute sections of the show page that appears after a successful page creation.

Running our new system spec, we get the following error:

```
1) Pages A new page can be added
   Failure/Error: visit new_admin_page_path

   NameError:
     undefined local variable or method `new_admin_page_path'
```

We can see that our spec is failing because it can't find a route for our new_admin_page_path. We need to add a route for this path but not in the usual way of modifying our routes.rb file. Active Admin adds routes for us if we use the ActiveAdmin.register method to register a new model. In our app/admin directory, let's create a new file called pages.rb with the following content:

```
ActiveAdmin.register Page do
end
```

This gives us a new route for our `new_admin_page_path` and moves us along to our next spec failure message:

```
1) Pages A new page can be added
   Failure/Error: fill_in 'Tags', with: 'foo, bar'

   Capybara::ElementNotFound:
     Unable to find field "Tags" that is not disabled
```

This error is telling us that Capybara can't find a form field with the label of `"Tags"`. We need to add a form field for our `tags_string` attribute. Unfortunately, Active Admin doesn't have an easy way to add a single form field to the existing form fields that it generates for us automatically. We will need to override the entire default form that Active Admin generates for us.

Let's modify our `admin/pages.rb` file to add a custom form:

```
form do |f|
  f.semantic_errors
  inputs do
    f.input :user
    f.input :title
    f.input :summary
    f.input :content
    f.input :tags_string, label: 'Tags'
    f.input :published
  end
  f.actions
end
```

This gets our `tags_string` form field to show up and also allows us to customize our form if we needed any other customizations. Now when we run our spec, we get the following error:

```
1) Pages A new page can be added
   Failure/Error: raise ActiveModel::ForbiddenAttributesError ...

   ActiveModel::ForbiddenAttributesError:
     ActiveModel::ForbiddenAttributesError
```

We're getting this error because we have not yet permitted valid parameters to be processed. This is similar to how we have to permit parameters in our non-admin Rails controllers. We need to add a `permitted_params` method call and add our `Page` parameter list:

```
permit_params :user_id,
              :title,
              :summary,
              :content,
```

```
                   :tags_string,
                   :published
```

This allows our Active Admin to process the parameters that we're passing in from our form. Now when we run our spec, we get the following error message:

```
1) Pages A new page can be added
    Failure/Error: expect(page).to have_css('td', text: 'bar, foo')
      expected to find css "td" within #<Capybara::Node::Element ...
```

The page we land on after a successful Page creation is the Active Admin equivalent of a Rails show page for our Page model. We can see that the tags_string attribute is not being displayed. We have a similar situation as before with our Active Admin generated form; we need to customize the show page output to display our tags_string attribute.

Overriding Active Admin Form Field Values

Our tags_string field is not being populated with the existing tag values. We can run our spec using SHOW_CHROME=1 to confirm. The missing values make sense because tags_string is an attr_accessor attribute on our Page model and not an actual ActiveRecord database column.

We can fix this by providing the value ourselves. First, we need a helper method to convert our tags attribute into a comma-separated string. Let's add a spec to capture this idea. In our spec/models/page_spec.rb file, let's add the following spec:

```
describe '#tags_string_for_form' do
  let(:tag) { create(:tag, name: 'foo') }
  let(:tag2) { create(:tag, name: 'bar') }
  let(:page) { create(:page, :published) }

  before do
    create(:page_tag, page:, tag:)
    create(:page_tag, page:, tag: tag2)
  end

  it 'returns the tags in comma delimited format' do
    expect(page.tags_string_for_form).to eq('bar, foo')
  end
end
```

We then get our spec failure message:

```
1) Page#tags_string_for_form returns the tags in comma delimited
   format
    Failure/Error: expect(page.tags_string_for_form).to eq('bar, foo')
```

```
NoMethodError:
   undefined method `tags_string_for_form' for #<Page id: ...
```

Our failure message tells us we need to add a method to our Page model named tags_string_ for_form. Let's modify our app/models/page.rb file to add it:

```
def tags_string_for_form
end
```

When we re-run our spec, we get a different failure message:

```
1) Page#tags_string_for_form returns the tags in comma delimited
   format
   Failure/Error: expect(page.tags_string_for_form).to eq('bar, foo')

      expected: "bar, foo"
           got: nil
```

Let's modify our tags_string_for_form method to return the expected value:

```
def tags_string_for_form
  tags.ordered.map(&:name).join(', ')
end
```

We "*map over*" our ordered tags attribute, calling the name method on each tag to get the name of the tag. This results in an array that we can then join together using a comma. This final string is returned from our method.

When we re-run our spec, we can see it's now passing. Now we can modify our admin/pages.rb file to add a custom show page that uses our new tags_string_for_form method:

```
show do
  attributes_table do
    row :user
    row :title
    row :slug
    row :summary
    row :content
    row('Tags') { |p| p.tags_string_for_form }
    row :published
  end
end
```

This gets our tags appearing on the page and gets our spec passing. Next, let's add a spec for our ability to edit a page:

```ruby
describe 'An existing page' do
  let(:the_page) { create(:page, :published, user:) }
  let(:user2) { create(:user) }

  before do
    the_page.tags << create(:tag, name: 'foo')
    the_page.tags << create(:tag, name: 'bar')
    user2
  end

  it 'can be edited' do
    visit admin_root_path

    fill_in 'Email', with: user.email
    fill_in 'Password', with: 'changeme'
    click_button 'Submit'

    expect(page).to have_css('h2', text: 'Dashboard')

    visit admin_pages_path

    click_link 'Edit'

    expect(page).to have_select('page_user_id', selected: user.name)
    expect(page).to have_field('page_title', with: the_page.title)
    expect(page).to have_field('page_summary', with: the_page.summary)
    expect(page).to have_field('page_content', with: the_page.content)
    expect(page).to have_field('page_tags_string', with: 'bar, foo')
    expect(page).to have_unchecked_field('page_published')

    select user2.name, from: 'User'

    fill_in 'Title', with: 'Page Title'
    fill_in 'Summary', with: 'Summary info'
    fill_in 'Content', with: 'Content goes here'
    fill_in 'Tags', with: 'foo, bar, baz'

    check('Published')

    click_button('Update Page')

    within '.flashes' do
      text = 'Page was successfully updated.'
      expect(page).to have_css('.flash_notice', text:)
    end

    within '#main_content' do
      expect(page).to have_css('td', text: user2.name)
      expect(page).to have_css('td', text: 'Page Title')
      expect(page).to have_css('td', text: 'Summary info')
```

```
        expect(page).to have_css('td', text: 'Content goes here')
        expect(page).to have_css('span.yes', text: 'YES')
        expect(page).to have_css('td', text: 'bar, baz, foo')
      end
    end
end
```

When we run our new edit spec, we get the following error:

```
1) Pages An existing page can be edited
   Failure/Error: expect(page).to have_field('page_tags_string',
     with: 'bar, foo')
     expected to find visible field "page_tags_string" that is not
     disabled with value "bar, foo" but there were no matches.
```

Let's modify our admin/pages.rb file to use our tags_string_for_form method. We need to modify our form block to use the input_html attribute to set the value of our tags_string field:

```
f.input :tags_string, label: 'Tags',
  input_html: { value: f.object.tags_string_for_form }
```

We can access our Page object using the f.object method, and then we can call our tags_string_for_form method on that to get the comma-separated value we want.

The rest of the spec is a lot like our previous spec for creating a new page. When we run it again, we can see it is now passing, although we have created some code duplication along the way.

Factoring Out Duplicate Login Code

We're now logging in to our admin three times in two different spec files. It's time to factor out a helper method to reduce code duplication. Let's create a new directory in our spec directory named support, and inside our new directory, let's create a new file called login.rb. Then let's add a method to our new file to handle logging in:

```
def login_as(user)
  visit admin_root_path

  expect(page).to have_css('h2', text: 'Admin')
  expect(page).to have_css('h2', text: 'Sign in')

  fill_in 'Email', with: user.email
  fill_in 'Password', with: 'changeme'
  click_button 'Submit'
```

```
    expect(page).to have_css('h2', text: 'Dashboard')
  end
```

To give RSpec access to our new `login_as` method, we need to add the following line to the bottom of our `spec/rails_helper.rb` file:

```
require "#{Rails.root}/spec/support/login"
```

This will load our `login.rb` file whenever our spec suite is run.

Now we can replace our three login calls with a single call to our new helper method. The first one is in our `system/login_spec.rb` file:

```
require 'rails_helper'

RSpec.describe 'Login Page' do
  let(:user) { create(:user) }

  it 'Admin requires logging in' do
    login_as(user)

    click_link 'Logout'

    expect(page).to have_link 'My Blog'
  end
end
```

The other two are in our `system/admin/pages_spec.rb` file. Let's do a similar replacement on them. In fact, in all of our admin pages, we are going to need to log in before doing much else, so let's add our `login_as` call in a `before` block so it's called before every spec runs:

```
before do
  login_as(user)
end
```

Once we've done that, let's re-run our system specs and make sure they are all still passing:

```
SHOW_CHROME=1 be rspec spec/system/**/*.rb
```

Previewing a Page

Next, we're going to customize our `Page` admin, so we can visit a page directly from within our admin interface. We'll do this by adding a custom link to our `index` page. We don't yet have an index page spec, so let's start there. Let's add this new spec to our "An existing page" describe block in our `system/admin/pages_spec.rb` file:

```
it 'can be visited' do
  visit admin_pages_path

  within '.index_content' do
    expect(page).to have_css('td', text: the_page.title)
    expect(page).to have_css('td', text: 'bar, foo')
    expect(page).to have_css('span.yes', text: 'YES')

    new_window = window_opened_by do
      click_link("/pages/#{the_page.slug}")
    end

    within_window new_window do
      expect(page).to have_css('h2', text: the_page.title)
    end
  end
end
```

To start with, we visit our `Page` index page. Then we use the `within` method to limit our scope to the `.index_content` element. This is the element that contains our table of `Page` objects. We can then use the `have_css` matcher to check that our `Page` is listed in the table.

Next, we use the `window_opened_by` method to open a new window when we click our `Page` link. We then use the `within_window` method to switch to that new window and check that it contains our `Page` title.

Let's run our spec and see what happens:

```
1) Pages An existing page can be visited
   Failure/Error: expect(page).to have_css('td', text: 'bar, foo')
```

Right away, we can see that we are going to need to fully customize our index page to show our tags. Let's do that now by adding a new `index` block to our `ActiveAdmin.register` call in our `admin/pages.rb` file:

```
index do
  column :title
  column('Tags') { |p| p.tags_string_for_form }
end
```

This change breaks our ability to click the "Edit" link, and that breaks a previously working spec, but we'll get it fixed up momentarily.

The spec failure we're concerned with at the moment is the complaint about our `published` column:

```
1) Pages An existing page can be visited
   Failure/Error: expect(page).to have_css('span.yes', text: 'YES')
     expected to find css "span.yes"
```

Let's fix that by adding a new `published` column to our `index` block:

```
column :published
```

Our next spec failure message complains about our link to visit our `Page`:

```
) Pages An existing page can be visited
  Failure/Error: click_link("/pages/#{the_page.slug}")

  Capybara::ElementNotFound:
    Unable to find link
```

Let's fix that by adding a link to our non-admin show page. In our `index` block, we can add a new column with a block that returns a link to the public URL of our page:

```
column('Preview') do |p|
  path = "/page/#{p.slug}"
  link_to path, path, target: '_blank'
end
```

If we now run our whole spec file, we can see that we've broken a previous spec. Our `edit` link is no longer working:

```
1) Pages An existing page can be edited
   Failure/Error: click_link 'Edit'

   Capybara::ElementNotFound:
     Unable to find link "Edit"
```

When we customized the columns in our `index` block, we accidentally removed our default `Edit` link. Let's add it back in, as well as the `id` column and our batch actions checkbox:

```
index do
  selectable_column
  id_column
  column :title
  column('Tags') { |p| p.tags_string_for_form }
  column :published
  column('Preview') do |p|
    path = "/page/#{p.slug}"
    link_to path, path, target: '_blank'
  end
  actions
end
```

Our Active Admin `Page` index is back to a fully working state, and all of our specs should be back to passing now.

Managing Images

The next piece of functionality we're going to add to our admin is the ability to manage our image uploads. We'll want to be able to upload images, edit them, and delete them. We'll also want to provide a thumbnail of an uploaded image as well as a valid HTML `<image />` tag that we can easily use in our `Page` content.

Viewing Images

Let's start by adding a new spec that tests our ability to view images in our admin, in a new `Images` index page. In our `system/admin` directory, let's add a new file called `images_spec.rb` with the following content:

```
require 'rails_helper'

RSpec.describe 'Images' do
  let(:user) { create(:user) }
  let(:img) { Image.last }

  before do
    login_as(user)
  end

  describe 'index' do
    before do
      create(:image)
    end
```

```
it 'renders images' do
  visit admin_images_path

  within 'table.index_table' do
    within 'td.col-name' do
      expect(page).to have_text(img.name)
    end

    within 'td.col-image' do
      xpath = <<~IMG.squish
        //img[@height='80' and
          @alt='#{img.name}' and
          @title='#{img.name}' and
          @src='/images/#{img.id}']
      IMG
      expect(page).to have_xpath(xpath)
    end

    within 'td.col-image_tag' do
      text = <<~IMG.squish
        <img alt="#{img.name}"
             title="#{img.name}"
             src="/images/#{img.id}" />
      IMG
      expect(page).to have_text(text)
    end
  end
end
end
```

We'll test that our admin images index has columns for the image name, a valid thumbnail image, and a valid HTML <image /> tag. We'll also test that the image name is displayed as the alt and title attributes of the image in our thumbnail and in our <image /> tag.

We're using within blocks to limit our scope to the exact td tags where we expect to find things. We need to do it this way because our image name is present as a string in one form or another in all three of the columns we're testing.

We are using Capybara's has_xpath matcher to test that our thumbnail image is displayed on our page as properly rendered HTML. We then use Capybara's has_text matcher to test that a non-rendered string representation of our <image /> tag is displayed on the page as well. This second version can be used to easily copy and paste the <image /> tag into our Page content later when we're making new pages.

Let's run our spec and see what happens:

```
1) Images index renders images
   Failure/Error: visit admin_images_path
```

```
NameError:
    undefined local variable or method `admin_images_path'
```

As before, the admin route we're trying to access does not yet exist. We can get the route working by simply adding a new Active Admin file with a proper `ActiveAdmin.register` block for our `Image` model. Let's do that now. In our `app/admin` directory, let's add a new file called `images.rb` with the following content:

```
ActiveAdmin.register Image do
end
```

Re-running our spec, we can see that we've got our Admin Image routes now, and we have a new failure message:

```
1) Images index renders images
   Failure/Error:
   ...

   Capybara::ElementNotFound:
     Unable to find css "td.col-image"
```

This error message is telling us that we're not able to find a `td` tag with the class `col-image`. Let's fix that by adding a custom `index` block to our `ActiveAdmin.register` block and a `column` for our image:

```
index do
  column 'Image' do |i|
    image_tag image_path(i),
      height: 80,
      alt: i.name,
      title: i.name
  end
end
```

We're using the Rails `image_tag` helper and our `image_path` route to create a thumbnail image with a height of 80 pixels that we can use to preview our full-size image. We're also using the image name field to set the `alt` and `title` attributes of our image.

Let's run our spec again and see what happens:

```
1) Images index renders images
   Failure/Error:
   ...
```

```
Capybara::ElementNotFound:
  Unable to find css "td.col-name"
```

To get this failure fixed, we need to add a `column` for our image name. Let's do that now:

```
index do
  column :name
  column 'Image' do |i|
    image_tag image_path(i),
      height: 80,
      alt: i.name,
      title: i.name
  end
end
```

This moves us to our next failure message:

```
1) Images index renders images
   Failure/Error:
   ...

   Capybara::ElementNotFound:
     Unable to find css "td.col-image_tag"
```

This failure message is telling us that we're not able to find a `td` tag with a CSS class `col-image_tag`. This is our table column where we want to display our HTML `<image />` tag. Let's add a `column`; it will be similar to our thumbnail column except that we will display the `<image />` tag itself, not a rendered HTML image:

```
column 'Image Tag' do |i|
  "#{image_tag image_path(i), alt: i.name, title: i.name}"
end
```

This gets our spec passing.

Because we added a custom `index` block to our `ActiveAdmin.register` block, we've lost some of the default columns that Active Admin provides: `selectable_column`, `id_column`, and `actions`. Let's add them back in:

```
index do
  selectable_column
  id_column
  column :name
  column 'Image' do |i|
```

```
    image_tag image_path(i),
      height: 80,
      alt: i.name,
      title: i.name
  end
  column 'Image Tag' do |i|
    "#{image_tag image_path(i), alt: i.name, title: i.name}"
  end
  actions
end
```

We created our spec using a factory for our image. We will also want to be able to upload new images via a regular HTML form.

Uploading New Images

Our inclusion of Active Storage into our blog application takes care of the image file storage work for us; it will use whatever we defined in our `storage.yml` file. We just need to add an image upload form to facilitate uploading the image from our local machine to our application.

Our spec to capture our image upload functionality is

```
describe 'new' do
  it 'uploads an image' do
    visit new_admin_image_path

    fill_in 'Name', with: 'Name'
    file = Rails.root.join('spec/factories/images/image.jpeg')
    attach_file 'Image', file
    click_button 'Create Image'

    within '.flashes' do
      expect(page).to have_css('.flash_notice',
        text: 'Image was successfully created.')
    end

    within '.image table' do
      within 'tr.row-name td' do
        expect(page).to have_text(img.name)
      end

      within 'tr.row-image td' do
        xpath = <<~IMG.squish
          //img[@height='80' and
            @alt='#{img.name}' and
            @title='#{img.name}' and
            @src='/images/#{img.id}']
        IMG
        expect(page).to have_xpath(xpath)
      end
```

```
      within 'tr.row-image_tag td' do
        text = <<~IMG.squish
          <img alt="#{img.name}"
               title="#{img.name}"
               src="/images/#{img.id}" />
        IMG
        expect(page).to have_text(text)
      end
    end
  end
end
```

We want to upload an image and also give it a friendly name for use with our HTML `alt` and `title` attributes. We use Capybara's `attach_file` helper method to attach our image file to our form. This mimics navigating to the file on our local computer and selecting it for upload. We pass the `attach_file` method the file path to our image file using Rails' `.root` method as the base of our path.

After a successful upload, we expect to see a flash message indicating that our image was successfully created. We also expect to see our image name, thumbnail image, and image tag in our table. These are similar to the expectations we have for our `index` spec, the major difference being that the CSS class names are mostly on the `<tr>` tags instead of the `<td>` tags.

Running our new spec, we get the following failure message:

```
1) Images new uploads an image
   Failure/Error: attach_file 'Image', file

   Capybara::ElementNotFound:
     Unable to find file field "Image"
```

Our failure message is telling us that Capybara is unable to find an Image file field on our form. Apparently, Active Admin doesn't understand our `has_one_attached` association we added to our `Image` model. We can fix this by adding a custom form block to our `ActiveAdmin.register` block and adding an `f.input` for our `image` field:

```
form do |f|
  f.inputs do
    f.input :name
    f.input :image
  end
  f.actions
end
```

And since we're adding a custom form block that overrides Active Admin's default form block, we need to add our `name` field and the Active Admin `actions` method also.

When we run our spec again, we get a different failure message:

```
1) Images new uploads an image
   Failure/Error: raise ActiveModel::ForbiddenAttributesError
     if !attributes.permitted?

   ActiveModel::ForbiddenAttributesError:
     ActiveModel::ForbiddenAttributesError
```

This failure message is telling us that we're trying to pass attributes to our Image model that are not permitted. This is similar to how Rails handles strong parameters in a regular controller. We can fix this by adding the Active Admin equivalent of allowing expected parameters to our ActiveAdmin.register block:

```
permit_params :name, :image
```

This fixes our permitted parameters failure message. We now get a different failure message:

```
1) Images new uploads an image
   Failure/Error:
   ...

   Capybara::ElementNotFound:
     Unable to find css "tr.row-image td"
```

In Active Admin, after we successfully create a new record, we are redirected to the show page for that record. To get our spec passing, we need to add a custom show block to our ActiveAdmin.register block and customize the rows, just like how we customized the columns for our index block:

```
show do
  attributes_table do
    row :name
    row 'Image' do |i|
      image_tag image_path(i),
        height: 80,
        alt: i.name,
        title: i.name
    end
    row 'Image Tag' do |i|
      "#{image_tag image_path(i), alt: i.name, title: i.name}"
    end
  end
end
```

This gets our spec passing. We can now upload images to our application, and we see an image thumbnail and image tags in our `index` and `show` pages.

We also created some code duplication in our specs.

Factor Out Our Image Matchers

Let's factor out our thumbnail image and image tag matchers into helper methods:

```ruby
private

def thumbnail_xpath(img)
  <<~IMG.squish
    //img[@height='80' and
      @alt='#{img.name}' and
      @title='#{img.name}' and
      @src='/images/#{img.id}']
  IMG
end

def image_tag_string(img)
  <<~IMG.squish
    <img alt="#{img.name}"
        title="#{img.name}"
        src="/images/#{img.id}" />
  IMG
end
```

Then we can replace the locations in our specs where we were using these matchers within our helper methods, first in our `index` spec:

```ruby
within 'td.col-image' do
  expect(page).to have_xpath(thumbnail_xpath(img))
end

within 'td.col-image_tag' do
  expect(page).to have_text(image_tag_string(img))
end
```

And then also in our `show` spec:

```ruby
within 'tr.row-image td' do
  expect(page).to have_xpath(thumbnail_xpath(img))
end

within 'tr.row-image_tag td' do
  expect(page).to have_text(image_tag_string(img))
end
```

We can undoubtedly factor things down further, but we risk making things harder to understand and more difficult to work on in the future. There is a balance to be had between reducing code duplication and making things too abstract. You'll find that balance for yourself, or with your team, the more code you write.

We can now upload images into our application. We will obviously want to be able to modify our images too.

Editing Images

As far as our Active Admin code is concerned, modifying images is very similar to creating images. Our `ActiveAdmin.register` block will use our existing custom `form` and `show` blocks when adding new or editing existing image uploads.

Let's add a spec for editing an image:

```ruby
describe 'edit' do
  let(:name) { 'New Name' }

  before do
    create(:image)
  end

  it 'updates an image' do
    visit edit_admin_image_path(img)

    within 'form.image' do
      within '.inline-hints' do
        expect(page).to have_xpath(thumbnail_xpath(img))
      end
    end

    fill_in 'Name', with: name
    file = Rails.root.join('spec/factories/images/image.jpeg')
    attach_file 'Image', file
    click_button 'Update Image'

    within '.flashes' do
      expect(page).to have_css('.flash_notice',
        text: 'Image was successfully updated.')
    end

    img.reload

    within '.image table' do
      within 'tr.row-name td' do
        expect(page).to have_text(name)
      end

      within 'tr.row-image td' do
        expect(page).to have_xpath(thumbnail_xpath(img))
      end
```

```
      within 'tr.row-image_tag td' do
        expect(page).to have_text(image_tag_string(img))
      end
    end
  end
end
```

We first create an image record in our database using our image factory. We don't need to assign the created image to a local variable because we can use the img from our let at the top of our file, where it gets the last image created.

Next, we visit the edit page for our image. On the page, we expect to see a thumbnail of our image. This isn't strictly necessary, but it's a good sanity check to make sure we're on the right page and that we're about to modify the image that we mean to modify. We then fill in the name field with our new name. We've created this static name string in a let block so that we can use it in multiple places in our spec, and additionally if we change it later, then we only need to modify a single code location.

We then attach a new image file to our form. We again use the attach_file method. We click the *Update Image* button and check for our success message.

If everything has gone as planned, we next need to reload our image record from our database. This is because Active Admin will have updated our image record in our database, but our local img variable will still be pointing to the old record, with the old name and image data. We then check that our show page has our new image name and that our image thumbnail and image tag are both correct.

Running this spec gives us a failure message:

```
1) Images edit updates an image
   Failure/Error:
     within '.inline-hints' do
       expect(page).to have_xpath(thumbnail_xpath(img))
     end

   Capybara::ElementNotFound:
     Unable to find css ".inline-hints"
```

This is failing because we haven't added any code to our form block to display the image thumbnail. Active Admin has the concept of a form field hint which can be whatever we would like to display below our form field. We just need to add a hint option to our f.input image field:

```
form do |f|
  hint = image_tag image_path(f.object),
                    height: 80,
                    alt: f.object.name,
                    title: f.object.name

  inputs do
    f.input :name
    f.input :image, as: :file, hint:
```

```
    end
    f.actions
end
```

This will display our image thumbnail below our image field in our form. We can run our spec again and see that it passes. We can also see when we run our previous specs that we broke one of them:

```
1) Images new uploads an image
   Failure/Error:
     hint = image_tag image_path(f.object),
                       height: 80,
                       alt: f.object.name,
                       title: f.object.name

   ActionView::Template::Error:
     No route matches {:action=>"show", :controller=>"images",
       :id=>nil}, missing required keys: [:id]
```

What happened? Well, remember that when we render our Active Admin image upload form, it's the same form fields for both our new and edit routes; the only differences are our <form> attributes. This means the hint we have created is trying to display a thumbnail of an image that doesn't exist yet in our database and therefore does not yet have an id assigned. The evidence is in the error message, where we see the id parameter is set to nil:

```
No route matches {:action=>"show", :controller=>"images", :id=>nil}
```

We can fix this by adding a conditional suffix to our hint:

```
hint = image_tag image_path(f.object),
                  height: 80,
                  alt: f.object.name,
                  title: f.object.name if f.object.persisted?
```

So now we can support both scenarios, when we have an image that already exists in our database and also when we are creating a new image. We have also created more code duplication. Time to refactor.

Factor Out Duplicate Expectations

Two of our specs now have the same show page expectations. We can factor them out into a shared method. We also have the option of using a shared example group, but for this small amount of code, it's probably not worth the complexity and additional indirection that it would introduce for our future selves. Let's add a method to our spec:

```
private

def validate_show_page(img)
  within '.image table' do
    within 'tr.row-name td' do
      expect(page).to have_text(img.name)
    end

    within 'tr.row-image td' do
      expect(page).to have_xpath(thumbnail_xpath(img))
    end

    within 'tr.row-image_tag td' do
      expect(page).to have_text(image_tag_string(img))
    end
  end
end
```

We can then replace our duplicate code in our new spec:

```
describe 'new' do
  it 'uploads an image' do
    ...
    within '.flashes' do
      expect(page).to have_css('.flash_notice',
        text: 'Image was successfully created.')
    end

    validate_show_page(img)
  end
end
```

And also in our edit spec:

```
describe 'edit' do
  let(:name) { 'New Name' }

  before do
    create(:image)
  end

  it 'updates an image' do
    ...
    img.reload
```

```
      validate_show_page(img)
   end
end
```

If you like, you can also factor out our image file path into a small helper method:

```
private

def file_path
  Rails.root.join('spec/factories/images/image.jpeg')
end
```

Deleting Images

I've found through experience supporting users that building ways to delete data into an application isn't always a good idea. Just as soon as you provide this functionality, someone will use it accidentally, and then you'll have to spend time restoring the deleted data from backups or creating it brand new again if you don't yet have backups.

You are creating backups, right?

However you work this out with your own data, in our case we're going to embrace our Active Admin delete functionality, mostly because it's a good learning experience. We'll encounter the need to confirm a destructive action with Capybara, so that will be fun.

Let's add a spec for deleting an image. The delete functionality and link is already built into Active Admin and is already present on our `index` page as well as our `show` page. We just need to add a spec to test it. I would imagine most image deletions will take place from the `index` page, so let's add our spec there inside our existing `describe 'index'` block:

```
it 'deletes an image' do
  visit admin_images_path

  accept_confirm do
    click_link 'Delete'
  end

  within '.flashes' do
    expect(page).to have_css('.flash_notice',
      text: 'Image was successfully destroyed.')
  end
end
```

The exciting thing here is the `accept_confirm` method. This is a Capybara helper method that wraps our `click_link` call and will accept the resulting confirmation dialog that is displayed. We can run our spec and see that it passes and that we do get a success message.

Figure 13-2 Active Admin image filters

Admin Filters

Active Admin provides filters to search our data on the `index` page for any type of record we register. This is great except that the default filtering includes all of our fields, which is not always desirable. For example, right now, on our `Images` page we have the filters shown in Figure 13-2 available and turned on by default.

We can configure which fields are available for filtering by adding `filter` entries. So if we wanted to get rid of the image attachment filter and the image blob filters, we could do this by adding only the filters that we do want to be present into our `ActiveAdmin.register` block:

```
ActiveAdmin.register Image do
  filter :name
  filter :created_at
  filter :updated_at
  ...
end
```

If we have a lot of default filters that we do want to keep and only a few that we want to remove, we can instead use the different Active Admin `remove_filter` syntax:

```
ActiveAdmin.register Image do
  remove_filter :image_blob, :image_attachment

  # other code not shown for brevity
end
```

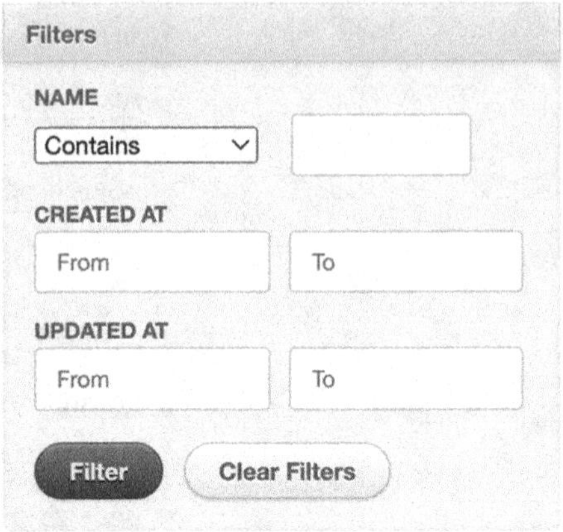

Figure 13-3 Fewer
Active Admin image filters

Either of these options will result in only the filters we want to be available on our index page to appear, as shown in Figure 13-3.

Let's also remove an unnecessary filter from our Pages admin page:

```
remove_filter :page_tags
```

We would never filter pages by join table data, so this makes sense.

Our Active Admin filter customizations are minimal, so we will not write any specs for them. It's also highly unlikely we will remove the name, created_at, or updated_at fields from our image table anytime soon. Feel free to add specs for your own blog application filters if you like.

Managing Users

We've now seen how to manage our Image and Page models with Active Admin. Now we'll see how to manage our User model. The main functionality this addition provides is the ability to create users and then be able to update their passwords and email addresses. You may not find this useful as a single administrator for a one-user blog application, but this will likely be the smallest Rails application you ever work on in your entire software engineering career, hopefully.

Adding New Users

Let's add a spec for creating a new user. We'll add this new spec into a new file called users_spec.rb located in our spec/system/admin directory:

```
require 'rails_helper'

RSpec.describe 'Users' do
  let(:user) { create(:user) }

  before do
```

```
      login_as(user)
  end

  describe 'A new user' do
    it 'can be added' do
      visit new_admin_user_path

      fill_in 'Name', with: 'Foo Bar'
      fill_in 'Email', with: 'foo@bar.com'
      fill_in 'user[password]', with: 'changeme'
      fill_in 'user[password_confirmation]', with: 'changeme'

      click_button 'Create User'

      within '.flashes' do
        text = 'User was successfully created.'
        expect(page).to have_css('.flash_notice', text:)
      end

      within '#main_content' do
        expect(page).to have_css('td', text: 'Foo Bar')
        expect(page).to have_css('td', text: 'foo@bar.com')
      end
    end
  end
end
```

There are no real surprises here. The only remarkable change from our previous Active Admin specs is that we cannot use `fill_in` with the HTML label of *Password* because given that we will also have a *Password Confirmation* field label on the form, the *Password* label is not unique. Instead, we have to use the HTML names of our fields, which are `user[password]` and `user[password_confirmation]`.

When we run this spec, we see that it fails:

```
1) Users A new user can be added
   Failure/Error: visit new_admin_user_path

   NameError:
     undefined local variable or method `new_admin_user_path'
```

The failure message indicates that we need to add a route for our new user path. We can do that by creating a new file called `users.rb` in our `app/admin` directory:

```
ActiveAdmin.register User do
end
```

This gets us our route and moves us on to our next failure:

```
1) Users A new user can be added
   Failure/Error: fill_in 'user[password]', with: 'changeme'

   Capybara::ElementNotFound:
     Unable to find field "user[password]" that is not disabled
```

This may seem confusing at first; we can set the password field in our `User` model, and we already have specs that prove it. The problem is that Active Admin does not automatically include attributes, and recalling back to our `User` model, our `password` attribute is not an actual field in our database, it is an `attr_reader`.

We can fix this by overriding the default `form` method in our Active Admin *User* registration block:

```
ActiveAdmin.register User do
  form do |f|
    f.semantic_errors
    inputs do
      f.input :name
      f.input :email
      f.input :password
      f.input :password_confirmation
    end
    f.actions
  end
end
```

Remember, if we override our `form` block, we have to add all the fields we want to be included in the form, so we're adding our `password` and `password_confirmation` fields as well as our `name` and `email` fields. We can now run our spec again and see that we have a new failure:

```
1) Users A new user can be added
   Failure/Error: raise ActiveModel::ForbiddenAttributesError if
   !attributes.permitted?

   ActiveModel::ForbiddenAttributesError:
     ActiveModel::ForbiddenAttributesError
```

We've seen this error message before. It means that we have not yet permitted our submitted form parameters. We can fix this error by adding them:

```
permit_params :name,
              :email,
```

```
                :password,
                :password_confirmation
```

This gets our spec to pass. We can now add a spec for updating an existing user record:

```
describe 'An existing user' do
  it 'can be updated' do
    visit admin_users_path

    click_link 'Edit'

    expect(page).to have_field('user_name', with: user.name)
    expect(page).to have_field('user_email', with: user.email)

    fill_in 'Name', with: 'Bar Baz'
    fill_in 'Email', with: 'bar@baz.com'
    fill_in 'user[password]', with: 'change_me'
    fill_in 'user[password_confirmation]', with: 'change_me'

    click_button('Update User')

    within '.flashes' do
      text = 'User was successfully updated.'
      expect(page).to have_css('.flash_notice', text:)
    end

    within '#main_content' do
      expect(page).to have_css('td', text: 'Bar Baz')
      expect(page).to have_css('td', text: 'bar@baz.com')
    end
  end
end
```

This spec passes with no changes. We're reusing the same form and parameters as we did for creating a new user, so we don't need to make any changes to our Active Admin registration block. Normally, I would never trust a spec that I didn't see fail at least once, but this spec is very simple, and it reuses the same patterns we've seen work in other specs, so I'm going to trust it.

Deleting Users

Since we can add and edit users, we should add a spec for deleting users too:

```
it 'can be deleted' do
  visit admin_users_path

  accept_confirm do
    click_link 'Delete'
```

```
  end

  within '.flashes' do
    expect(page).to have_css('.flash_notice',
      text: 'User was successfully destroyed.')
  end
end
```

This spec also passes with no changes to our Active Admin registration block. Similar to before, this spec is again very simple, and it reuses the same patterns we've seen work in other specs, so I'm again going to trust it.

Right now, our `index` and `show` pages are displaying all of our user attributes, including our `password_salt` and `password_hash` fields. Displaying these fields is not useful, so let's remove them by overriding our `index` and `show` blocks with just the fields we do want to display:

```
index do
  selectable_column
  id_column
  column :name
  column :email
  actions
end

show do
  attributes_table do
    row :name
    row :email
  end
end
```

Our user filter block is also displaying all of our user attributes, so let's remove the `password_salt` and `password_hash` fields from there too.

```
remove_filter :password_salt, :password_hash
```

Summary

This concludes our Active Admin chapter. I've shown enough of the basics to get you started with specs for your own Active Admin implementations. You probably want to add an Active Admin interface for managing page tags as well. I'm going to leave that as a TDD exercise for you to complete on your own.

Odds and Ends

14

This chapter will cover some additions and enhancements to our existing work:

1. Build a sitemap
2. Add pagination for our blog entries
3. Add CSS styling
4. Add syntax highlighting for code blocks

Build a Sitemap

A *sitemap* isn't a hard requirement for a website, but it is a good idea to have one. A sitemap is a URL endpoint, usually living at /sitemap.xml, that is available through a GET request and that lists all of the other URL endpoints on the website. A sitemap helps search engines find all of the pages in the website more easily compared to doing a full website crawl. For a large website, it can also help the search engine understand the hierarchical structure.

Let's add a sitemap to our blog application. To start with, we will add a request spec that will request the /sitemap.xml and verify that it is returning a valid XML response. Let's add the following to our spec/requests/home_spec.rb file:

```
describe 'GET /sitemap' do
  it 'returns http success' do
    get sitemap_path(format: :xml)
    expect(response).to be_successful
  end
end
```

Running this spec will result in a failure message because we don't yet have a route for
/sitemap.xml:

```
1) Home Page GET /sitemap returns http success
   Failure/Error: get sitemap_path(format: :xml)

   NoMethodError:
     undefined method `sitemap_path'
```

Let's add a route for this URL in our config/routes.rb file:

```
get 'sitemap', to: 'home#sitemap'
```

Re-running our spec moves us to our next error message:

```
1) Home Page GET /sitemap returns http success
   Failure/Error: get sitemap_path(format: :xml)

   AbstractController::ActionNotFound:
     The action 'sitemap' could not be found for HomeController
```

As suggested by the error message, let's add a sitemap action to our HomeController:

```
def sitemap
end
```

This gets our new request spec to pass. Next, we should parse the XML response and verify that it
contains our expected URLs. We can use Nokogiri to parse our XML response body and collect the
URL paths into an array, then we can easily check the contents of the array for known URL paths.

Before we pursue this, we should consider the XML structure of our sitemap and what it should
look like. We can find the standard XML structure for a sitemap published online at

www.sitemaps.org/protocol.html

Notice the <url> and <loc> are required fields. There are other optional fields available, but we
will stick with just the required fields for now. Our generated XML should look something like this:

```
<?xml version="1.0" encoding="UTF-8"?>
<urlset xmlns="http://www.sitemaps.org/schemas/sitemap/0.9">
<url>
  <loc>http://www.example.com/</loc>
</url>
</urlset>
```

Let's update our spec to parse the XML response and verify that it contains our expected URL paths:

```ruby
describe 'GET /sitemap' do
  let(:tag) { create(:tag) }
  let!(:page) do
    create(
      :page,
      :published,
      tags: [tag],
      created_at: '2023-02-19'
    )
  end

  it 'returns http success' do
    get sitemap_path(format: :xml)
    expect(response).to be_successful

    doc = Nokogiri::XML(response.body)
    urls = doc.css('loc').collect(&:text)
    paths = urls.map{ |url| URI.parse(url).path }

    expect(paths).to include(page_path(slug: page.slug))
  end
end
```

We're using the `Nokogiri::XML` method to parse the XML response body of our request into a Nokogiri document object. We then use the `doc`'s `css` method to find all of the `<loc>` elements and collect the URL (via the `text` field) of each `<loc>` element into an array. We then map over the array of URLs and extract the `path` portion of each URL using `URI.parse`. Finally, we can check that the array of paths includes the path for our page object we created using our `let!`.

When we run this spec, we get the following error message:

```
Failures:

1) Home Page GET /sitemap returns http success
   Failure/Error: expect(paths).to include(page_path ...
     expected [] to include "/page/page-title-1"
```

It looks like our `paths` array is empty, which makes sense because we have not yet implemented an ERB template for our `HomeController` sitemap action. Let's add an ERB template named `sitemap.xml.erb` in our `app/views/home` directory and add the following code to it:

```erb
<?xml version="1.0" encoding="UTF-8"?>
<urlset xmlns="http://www.sitemaps.org/schemas/sitemap/0.9">
<% Page.published.ordered.each do |p| -%>
<url>
  <loc><%= "http://127.0.0.1:3000/page/#{p.slug}" %></loc>
```

```
</url>
<% end -%>
</urlset>
```

This will generate sitemap XML that contains a `<url>` element for each published page in our database. We can now run our spec and see that it passes.

We probably do not want to hard-code the domain name and port number in our sitemap XML template. We should instead make it read from an environment variable and have a default value for when the environment variable is not set. Let's add this to our `sitemap` action in our `HomeController`:

```
def sitemap
  @url = ENV['BASE_URL'] || 'http://localhost:3000'
end
```

Then we can update our ERB template to use our new `@url` instance variable:

```
<% Page.published.ordered.each do |p| -%>
<url>
  <loc><%= "#{@url}/page/#{p.slug}" %></loc>
</url>
<% end -%>
```

Re-running our spec, we can see that it still passes. We of course need to make sure to set our new environment variable in our production environment, so don't forget!

Let's now add another expectation for our `Tag` URLs:

```
expect(paths).to include(tag_path(name: tag.name))
```

This fails as expected:

```
Failures:

1) Home Page GET /sitemap returns http success
   Failure/Error: expect(paths).to include(tag_path(name: tag.name))
     expected ["/page/page-title-1"] to include "/tag/name-1"
```

We can fix this error by adding a `<url>` element for each tag in our sitemap XML:

```erb
<% Tag.all.each do |t| -%>
<url>
  <loc><%= "#{@url}/tag/#{t.name}" %></loc>
</url>
<% end -%>
```

This gets our request spec back to passing.

The last thing we will add to our spec is an expectation for our sidebar archive links:

```ruby
expect(paths).to include('/search/2023/02')
```

This fails as expected:

```
Failures:

1) Home Page GET /sitemap returns http success
   Failure/Error: expect(paths).to include('/search/2023/02')
      expected ["/page/page-title-1", "/tag/name-1"] to
      include "/search/2023/02"
```

We can fix this error by adding a `<url>` element for each archive link in our sitemap XML:

```erb
<% Page.month_year_list.each do |i| %>
<url>
  <loc>
    <%= "#{@url}/search/#{i['year']}/#{i['month_number']}" %>
  </loc>
</url>
<% end %>
```

This gets our request spec back to passing. We can now do a bit of cleanup by moving our local variables into `let` statements:

```ruby
describe 'GET /sitemap' do
  let(:doc) { Nokogiri::XML(response.body) }
  let(:urls) { doc.css('loc').collect(&:text) }
  let(:paths) { urls.map{ |url| URI.parse(url).path } }
  let(:tag) { create(:tag) }
  let!(:page) do
    create(
      :page,
```

```
      :published,
      tags: [tag],
      created_at: '2023-02-19'
    )
  end

  it 'returns http success' do
    get sitemap_path(format: :xml)
    expect(response).to be_successful

    expect(paths).to include(page_path(slug: page.slug))
    expect(paths).to include(tag_path(name: tag.name))
    expect(paths).to include('/search/2023/02')
  end
end
```

We should re-run our spec to make sure it still passes.

Pagination

Once we have more than a handful of pages, we will want to add pagination. Pagination will allow our homepage to load faster, and our back-end database will not have to load as many records all at once for a given request. This will also be true for our tag pages and our search results pages.

Instead of inventing pagination from scratch, we will use the *Kaminari* gem. Kaminari is a pagination gem that is very easy to use and has a lot of options for customizing the look and feel of the pagination links.

Let's add the *Kaminari* gem to our `Gemfile`:

```
gem 'kaminari', '~> 1.2.2'
```

And then let's run the `bundle` command to install it:

```
bundle
```

Kaminari has a lot of options for customizing the look and feel of the pagination links. We can generate an initializer file for Kaminari, which contains all of the default options and values, by running the following command:

```
be rails g kaminari:config
```

We can then update the generated initializer file `kaminari_config.rb` values to our liking:

```ruby
# config/initializers/kaminari_config.rb

Kaminari.configure do |config|
  # config.default_per_page = 25
  # config.max_per_page = nil
  # config.window = 4
  # config.outer_window = 0
  # config.left = 0
  # config.right = 0
  # config.page_method_name = :page
  # config.param_name = :page
  # config.max_pages = nil
  # config.params_on_first_page = false
end
```

The defaults are fine for our purposes, so we will leave them as is for now.

Now that we have Kaminari installed, we can add pagination to our blog application. Thinking through it, we will want pagination on any page that displays a list of Page objects, so let's start with our homepage. We first need a spec to test the pagination functionality. Let's add the following to our `spec/system/home_spec.rb` file:

```ruby
describe 'pagination' do
  context 'with many pages' do
    it 'paginates' do
      create_list(:page, 26, :published)

      visit root_path

      articles = find_all('article')
      expect(articles.size).to eq(25)
      expect(page).to have_link('Next')
    end
  end
end
```

We begin this spec by calling FactoryBot's `create_list` method to create 26 published Page objects. This number of Page objects is just enough to trigger pagination to render since we have the Kaminari `default_per_page` set to 25 items per page. We then visit the homepage and expect to see exactly 25 Page objects (instead of 26). We then expect to find a "*Next*" link on the page. This will prove our pagination is being rendered on the homepage as expected.

When we run our spec, we get the following error:

```
1) Home pagination with many pages paginates
   Failure/Error: expect(articles.size).to eq(25)

     expected: 25
          got: 26
```

To fix this error, we need to add a `.page` call to our ActiveRecord query in our `HomeController` index method where we assign our `@pages` object. Let's update it to look like this:

```ruby
def index
  @pages = Page.published.ordered.page(params[:page])
end
```

When we re-run our spec, we get a new error message:

```
1) Home pagination with many pages paginates
   Failure/Error: expect(page).to have_link('Next')
     expected to find link "Next" but there were no matches
```

To fix this error, we need to add the pagination links to our homepage. You may recall that our `Page` objects are rendered in our shared partial template called `_pages.html.erb` residing in our `app/views/shared` directory.

Let's modify our partial to add a call to Kaminari's `paginate` method at the bottom of the page to render our pagination links:

```erb
<% pages.each do |page| %>
  <%= render partial: 'shared/page',
             locals: {
               page: page,
               content: page.summary
             } %>
<% end %>

<%= paginate pages %>
```

This gets our spec passing, and this is good, but we can do better.

Do we really need 26 `Page` objects to test our pagination? If we think about it, we really only need a few `Page` objects to test pagination. We need a couple of `Page` objects to render on our first page to exercise our render loop and then one more `Page` object to trigger pagination to render. Let's update our spec to only create three `Page` objects:

```
it 'paginates' do
  create_list(:page, 3, :published)

  visit root_path

  articles = find_all('article')
  expect(articles.size).to eq(2)
  expect(page).to have_link('Next')
end
```

This fails with the following error:

```
1) Home pagination with many pages paginates
   Failure/Error: expect(articles.size).to eq(2)

      expected: 2
           got: 3
```

Now we need to adjust our Kaminari initializer configuration to render only one Page object per page and only when we are running a spec. We can accomplish this by adding a conditional to our initializer file, to look at our Rails.env value and set our default_per_page to only 2 when we are in our test environment:

```
config.default_per_page = Rails.env.test? ? 2 : 25
```

This gets our spec passing again. Our system spec for our tags also needs to be updated to use pagination. Let's add a tag spec into our spec/system/tag_spec.rb file to test pagination:

```
describe 'pagination' do
  context 'with many tagged pages' do
    it 'paginates' do
      tag = create(:tag)
      create_list(:page, 3, :published)
      Page.all.each { |page| page.tags << tag }

      visit tag_path(name: tag.name)

      articles = find_all('article')
      expect(articles.size).to eq(2)
      expect(page).to have_link('Next')
    end
  end
end
```

This spec is very similar to the one we added to our homepage spec. We create a `Tag` object and then create three `Page` objects with our new tag assigned to each one. We then visit our tag show page and expect to see two `Page` objects and our "*Next*" link rendered.

When we run our new spec, we get the error:

```
Failure/Error: visit tag_path(name: tag.name)

ActionController::UrlGenerationError:
  No route matches {:action=>"show", :controller=>"tags", ...
```

This error is telling us that we need to add a route. We need to add our `Tag` show action route. Let's modify our `config/routes.rb` file to add this:

```
get 'tag/:name', to: 'tags#show', name: /[-a-z0-9_+]*/, as: :tag
```

This update moves us to our next error. When we run our spec again, we get

```
1) Tag displays clickable tags on a page
   Failure/Error: <%= paginate pages %>

   ActionView::Template::Error:
     undefined method `total_pages'
```

This error message may seem a bit cryptic at first, but we can assume the call to `paginate` is failing because we are not passing a Kaminari-like `page` object. We need to update our `TagsController` show method to call Kaminari's `page` method when we are retrieving our `Page` objects. Let's update our `show` method to look like this:

```ruby
def show
  tag = Tag.find_by(name: params[:name])
  redirect_to root_path and return unless tag

  @pages = tag.pages.published.ordered.page(params[:page])
end
```

This gets our spec passing.

The last bit of pagination we need to add is with our search. Let's add a spec to our `spec/system/search_spec.rb` file to test search results pagination:

```ruby
describe 'pagination' do
  context 'with many search result pages' do
    it 'paginates' do
```

```
      create_list(:page, 3, :published, content: 'foo bar baz')

      visit search_path(term: 'foo')

      articles = find_all('article')
      expect(articles.size).to eq(2)
      expect(page).to have_link('Next')
    end
  end
end
```

This spec fails in the same way as our tag spec:

```
1) Search Searching with a search term renders search results
   Failure/Error: <%= paginate pages %>

   ActionView::Template::Error:
     undefined method `total_pages'
```

The update for this failure is not going to be in the same location as with our previous controller updates. For searching, we use our `PageSearch` service class, so the fix will be in there instead of in our `SearchController` file. Let's update our `PageSearch` class to add our page call:

```
def self.search(params)
  return [] unless params.present?

  pages = if params[:year].present? && params[:month].present?
            Page.by_year_month(params[:year], params[:month])
          elsif params[:term].present?
            Page.by_term(params[:term])
          end

  return [] unless pages

  pages.published.ordered.page(params[:page])
end
```

This gets our spec passing. The reason we can't put the fix in the controller is because we sometimes return an empty array from our `search` method. An empty array does not respond to the `page` method, so we need to put the fix where we are returning actual `ActiveRecord Page` objects.

We could change our two early returns to use `Page.none` instead of returning an empty array, then we could put our `page` call in our controller. This is a matter of personal preference, so feel free to pursue that option if you like.

Fixing Specs

If we run our entire test suite now:

```
be rspec
```

we will see that our spec file `index.html.erb_spec.rb` located in our `spec/views/home` directory is failing:

```
1) home/index renders the page object
   Failure/Error: <%= paginate pages %>

   ActionView::Template::Error:
     undefined method `total_pages'
```

This is similar to our other pagination-related spec failures. We need to update our failing view spec to assign a properly paginated `Page` object, instead of an array. This will give us access to the `total_pages` method our view is trying, and failing, to call.

Let's update our spec to look like this:

```ruby
require 'rails_helper'

RSpec.describe 'home/index', type: :view do
  let!(:page) { create(:page) }

  it 'renders the page object' do
    assign(:pages, Page.page(1))
    render
    expect(rendered).to have_css('h2', text: page.title)
    expect(rendered).to have_css('p', text: page.created_at.to_fs)
    expect(rendered).to include(page.summary)
  end
end
```

The main change here is that we are now assigning a paginated `Page` object to our view instead of an array, but we also have to change our `let` to a `let!` that uses a `create` so that it is created before we perform our pagination `.page` call.

If we run our spec now, we will see that it is passing.

Styling

Without a doubt, we've paid very little attention to styling our application up to now. We now have a fully functioning application, so we can work to improve its appearance. As before, we are going to continue to use the Bootstrap CSS framework we installed previously.

CSS in Rails

When we generated our application using the rails new command, we passed in the option --css=bootstrap to choose Bootstrap as our CSS framework. This option caused our main application.scss file to be generated with the name application.boostrap.scss. I find having this longer filename serves no real purpose, and I prefer to rename it back to just the default application.scss filename. Let's do that now:

```
mv app/assets/stylesheets/application.bootstrap.scss \
   app/assets/stylesheets/application.scss
```

Renaming our application.scss file requires we also update the name in our package.json file. You might use a sed command to do this:

```
sed -i '' 's/\.bootstrap//g' package.json
```

Or just open our package.json file and change it manually.

Styling Our Public Pages

First, let's add styling to our _header.html.erb file, located in our app/views/shared directory. Let's add additional padding on the top and left side of our <header> container, using ps-1 and pt-1 to bring it down and to the right a bit. Right now, our link in our <h1> tag is underlined, so let's remove that by adding the text-decoration-none class.

Our updated file will look like this:

```
<header class="ps-1 pt-1">
  <h1>
    <%= link_to 'My Blog', root_path,
               class: 'text-decoration-none' %>
  </h1>
</header>
```

Now our header looks like Figure 14-1.

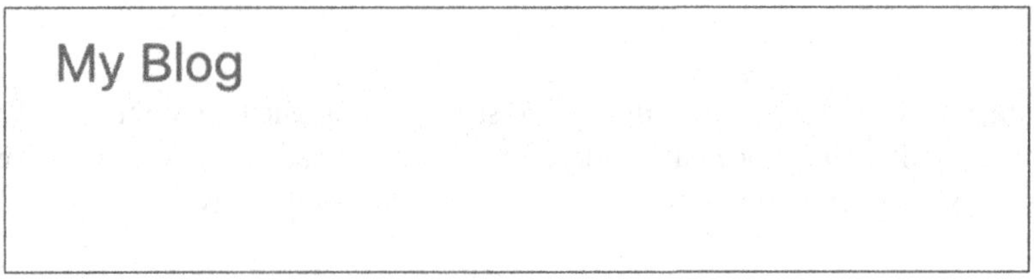

Figure 14-1 Header CSS

Figure 14-2 Page summary CSS

Next, let's add CSS styling to our _page.html.erb partial, located in our app/views/ shared directory. Let's give our <article> tag the card class, which will give it a rounded gray border as shown in Figure 14-2, and the p-3 and mb-3 classes to give it a bit of inner padding and bottom margin. Our updated file will look like this:

```
<article class="card p-3 mb-3">
  <h2><%= link_to page.title, page_path(slug: page.slug) %></h2>
  <p><%= page.created_at.to_fs %></p>
  <%= content.html_safe %>
  <p><%= tag_links(page.tags).html_safe %></p>
</article>
```

When we search our blog entries and get no results, we are rendering a *"No results found"* message in our index.html.erb file, found in our app/views/search directory. It's currently a bit tight against the left side of our page. Let's add the ps-2 class to give it more padding on the left side, as shown in Figure 14-3.

No results found

Figure 14-3 No search results CSS

Figure 14-4 Search form CSS

```
<% if @pages&.any? %>
  <%= render partial: 'shared/pages', locals: { pages: @pages } %>
<% else %>
  <p class="ps-2">No results found</p>
<% end %>
```

Now let's turn our attention to the sidebar section of our blog. First, let's add CSS styling to our `_search_form.html.erb` file, located in our `app/views/shared` directory. Let's join our search term text field and our search button together by adding the `input-group` class to our `<div>` container they live in. We also need to add the `form-control` class to our search term text field itself. And then let's also add the `btn` and `btn-primary` classes to our search button as shown in Figure 14-4. Our updated file will look like this:

```
<div>
  <%= form_for(:search, url: search_path, method: :get) do %>
    <div class="input-group">
      <input type="search" name="term" class="form-control" />
      <input type="submit" value="Search" class="btn btn-primary" />
    </div>
  <% end %>
</div>
```

Just below our search form, we have our *Archives* section which lives in our `_archives.html. erb` file in our `app/views/shared` directory. Like we did with our blog entries' `<article>` tag, let's add the `card` class to give it the same rounded gray border. Let's also add the `p-3` class to give it some inner padding and the `mt-3` class to give it some top margin, to push it down a bit from our search form.

Our archive list is currently decorated with the default list dots that are by default rendered with a `<ul>` tag. Let's remove those dots by adding the `list-unstyled` class to our `<ul>` tag. Let's also add the `pt-1` class to our `<li>` tags to give them a bit of top padding, to push them down from each other, as shown in Figure 14-5.

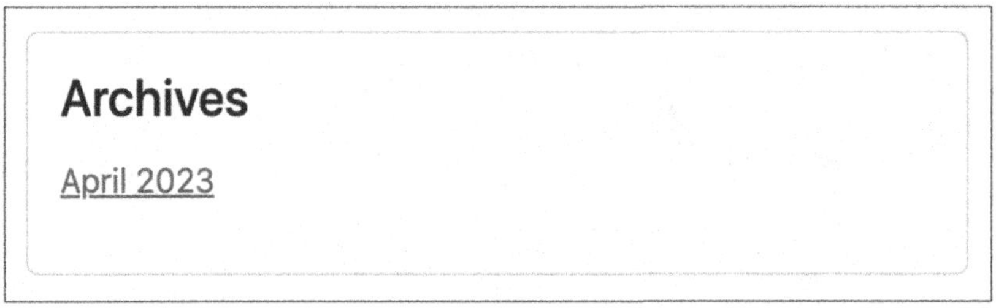

Archives

April 2023

Figure 14-5   Archive list CSS

Our updated file will look like this:

```
<div class="card p-3 mt-3">
  <h4>Archives</h4>
  <ul class="list-unstyled">
  <% Page.month_year_list.each do |item| %>
    <li class="pt-1">
      <%= link_to "#{item['month_name']} #{item['year']}",
                  "/search/#{item['year']}/#{item['month_number']}"
                  %>
    </li>
  <% end %>
  </ul>
</div>
```

The next bit of styling we will do is to our pagination links. Given the popularity of Bootstrap, and the fact that we're not creating the very first blog application that ever needed pagination styling, it's no surprise that there is already a Ruby gem to address our exact problem. The gem is called bootstrap5-kaminari-views, and it provides Bootstrap 5 styling for the kaminari pagination gem we're using.

Let's add the gem to our Gemfile:

```
gem 'bootstrap5-kaminari-views', '~> 0.0.1'
```

And then run bundle to install the gem.

To apply the styling, we need to modify our _pages.html.erb file located in our app/views/shared directory. We only need to pass the theme parameter with a value of 'bootstrap-5'. Our updated paginate call will look like this:

```
<%= paginate pages, theme: 'bootstrap-5' %>
```

This makes our pagination links, as shown in Figure 14-6, look similar to the other Bootstrap styles we are already using.

Figure 14-6 Pagination CSS

Styling Our Admin

The last bit of styling we will do is to style our Admin login page.

First, let's update our `admin.html.erb` layout file that is located in our `app/views/layouts` directory. Our `<h1>` tag is too tight against the top and left sides of the page. Let's add some extra margin:

```
<h1 class="ms-2 mt-1">Admin</h1>
```

The "*ms*" means "*margin start*" or left margin. The "*mt*" means "*margin top*" or top margin. The numeric suffix is the amount of margin with higher numbers being more margin than lower numbers.

Next, let's work on improving our login form. Let's open and modify our `new.html.erb` template file located in our `app/views/sessions` directory. We need to again add some left margin to our form; currently, it's too close to the left side of the page. Let's wrap our form in a `<div>` container and add the `ms-2` class to it:

```
<div class="ms-2">
...
</div>
```

To get our form fields looking a bit nicer, let's add the `form-control` class to each of them:

```
<%= f.email_field :email, class: 'form-control' %>
```

To add some space between our form fields, let's add the `mt-3` class to each of our `<div>` containers that wrap our form fields:

```
<div class="mt-3">
...
</div>
```

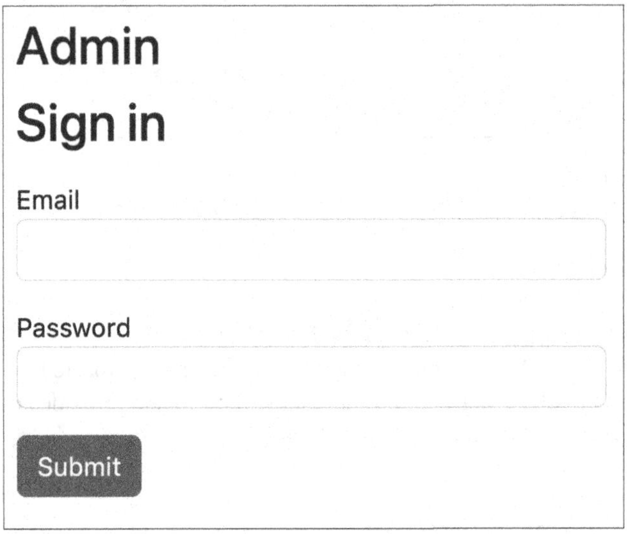

Figure 14-7   Admin login CSS

Next, let's improve our submit `<button>` by adding `"btn btn-primary"` classes to it:

```
<button type="submit" class="btn btn-primary">Submit</button>
```

Our form fields are looking better, but now they span the entire width of the page. Let's add a class to our `<div>` container to pull them in to about a fourth of the page. Bootstrap is based on a 12-column grid system, so 3 columns is a fourth of the page. Let's add the `col-3` class to our `<div>` container:

```
<div class="col-3 ms-2">
  ...
</div>
```

After our updates, our final `new.html.erb` file looks like this, and our login form looks like Figure 14-7:

```
<div class="col-3 ms-2">
  <%= form_for(:login, url: login_path) do |f| %>
    <h2>Sign in</h2>
    <div class="mt-3">
      <%= f.label :email %>
      <%= f.email_field :email, class: 'form-control' %>
    </div>
    <div class="mt-3">
      <%= f.label :password %>
      <%= f.password_field :password, class: 'form-control' %>
    </div>
```

```
      <div class="mt-3">
        <button type="submit" class="btn btn-primary">Submit</button>
      </div>
    <% end %>
</div>
```

Wrapping Up

This wraps up styling our blog application. We've added standard Bootstrap 5 styling to our blog application, and admittedly we could add a lot more. Bootstrap has lots of styling options, and we've only barely scratched the surface.

Code Highlighting

To close out this chapter, we're going to add code highlighting to our blog application. I'm assuming that you are reading this book because you are or soon will be a software engineer and that you will want to write blog entries that include code that you want to make syntax highlighted. If that's a wrong assumption, then you can skip this section.

We're going rogue here and will not be using a Ruby gem to do this. Instead, we're going to use a plain old JavaScript library called *Prism*:

https://prismjs.com/

Prism is a client-side syntax highlighting library that is very popular with software engineers and is used by many popular websites. It's also very easy to use. We're going to use the *Prism* library to highlight our <code> blocks in our blog entries.

The way it works is very simple. When we create a blog entry, and we include a <code> block in our HTML, we add a language-* CSS class to the <code> tag. For example, if we want to highlight a <code> block as Ruby code, we would add the language-ruby class to our <code> tag. After page load, Prism will look for classes it knows about and will highlight the <code> tag contents accordingly. Prism supports many different programming languages and has great support for Ruby.

Before we do anything else, let's add a new system spec, so we'll know when we have it working. In our spec/system directory, let's modify our existing page_spec.rb file to add this:

```ruby
describe 'syntax highlighting' do
  before do
    content = <<~RUBY.squish
      <pre>
        <code class="language-ruby">
          puts 'hello world!'
        </code>
      </pre>
    RUBY

    my_page.update(content:)
  end
```

```ruby
  it 'renders code blocks' do
    visit page_path(slug: my_page.slug)

    within 'pre' do
      expect(page).to have_text('puts')

      within 'code.language-ruby span.token.string' do
        expect(page).to have_text('hello world!')
      end
    end
  end
end
```

We're updating our existing my_page variable from the let at the top of the spec file to have a <code> block in its content field. Our <code> block contains a single line of Ruby code that outputs *hello world!*. We're then visiting our page and checking to see if our <code> tag is present and has the language-ruby class assigned. This is expected, even without Prism, but then we're checking to see if there is a <span> tag with CSS classes token and string that contains our string `hello world!`. We didn't add anything to do with <span> tags in our <code> block; that's what Prism does for us. So when we run our spec, and it begins to pass, we'll know our Prism setup is working.

Running our spec, we see that it fails, as expected. We need to install Prism into our application and configure it.

The first step is to visit the Prism website and download the JavaScript and CSS files. On this page, we can pick which languages we want to support and then download the files:

https://prismjs.com/download.html

Make sure and choose *Ruby* as one of the languages to support, then scroll to the bottom of the page and click each of the two *Download* buttons to download the JavaScript and CSS files. Move the prism.css CSS file into our app/assets/stylesheets directory and move the prism.js JavaScript file into our app/javascript directory.

Next, we need to load the prism.js JavaScript file into our application. Let's add this to the bottom of our app/javascript/application.js file:

```javascript
import './prism'
```

Our prism.js file is a plain old JavaScript file living in the same directory as our application.js file, so we can just import it into our application using a local path of "./". Notice how the file extension is not included in the import statement; it's optional and assumed to be .js.

Stimulus and Turbo

In our modern Rails application, we are by default using *Stimulus* and *Turbo*, mostly because we didn't say we didn't want to use them via the -skip-hotwire option when we created our application using the rails new command previously. But why am I writing about them?

Gone are the days of simply adding a `<script>` tag to our HTML to load a plain old JavaScript file. The modern way, especially inside a Rails application, is to use *Stimulus* to create a "*controller*" that is loaded into our HTML using "*data*" tags. Stimulus then *connects* and runs our JavaScript code only when and where we need it to. It's pretty fancy, especially if you're old enough to have ever supported IE6. But I digress.

To execute our Prism code, we need to add a *Stimulus* controller to our application. Let's create a new file in our `app/javascript/controllers` directory called `prism_controller.js` with this content:

```
import { Controller } from "@hotwired/stimulus"

export default class extends Controller {
  connect() {
    document.addEventListener('turbo:load', function() {
      Prism.highlightAll();
    });
  }
}
```

The point of this code is so that we call our `Prism.highlightAll()` method when the *Turbo* library has finished loading our page. Rails is using *Turbo* to load our pages, and it has a `turbo:load` event that we can listen for. When that event is fired, we know our page has finished loading, and we can then safely call our `Prism.highlightAll()` function.

But notice how this code is not stand-alone, it's wrapped inside a *Stimulus* controller `connect` method that is called when our Stimulus controller successfully connects to our HTML.

The next step is to add our new Stimulus controller to our list of all our Stimulus controllers. In our `app/javascript/controllers` directory, we need to modify our `index.js` file to add these two lines at the bottom:

```
import PrismController from "./prism_controller"
application.register("prism", PrismController)
```

This is very similar to adding a `<script>` tag to an HTML file, but instead of loading a JavaScript file, we're loading a Stimulus controller. The first line imports our `prism_controller.js` file, and the second line registers our controller with Stimulus and gives it the name `prism`.

The magic that connects our new Stimulus controller to our HTML is simply the proper naming of our Stimulus controller file and the presence of a `data-controller` attribute located somewhere in our HTML. We named our controller file `prism_controller.js`, and the part before the `_controller.js` is important for the next step.

Next, we need to decide where in our HTML we want to connect our Stimulus controller. We could load it at the top of every page, but that's a heavy-handed approach. We only want to load it on pages that have code blocks that need to be syntax highlighted, and we only want to execute it on blocks of HTML that need to be highlighted. So let's add our `data-controller` attribute to our `_page.html.erb` file, in our `<article>` tag:

```
<article class="card p-3 mb-3" data-controller="prism">
  <h2><%= link_to page.title, page_path(slug: page.slug) %></h2>
  <p><%= page.created_at.to_fs %></p>
  <%= content.html_safe %>
  <p><%= tag_links(page.tags).html_safe %></p>
</article>
```

With this modification, we're telling Stimulus to load our `prism` controller after our `<article>` tag is loaded. We're also telling Stimulus to connect our Prism controller to this particular block of HTML and then, if that is successful, to execute our `connect` method.

Now when we re-run our spec, it should pass. We've added the necessary JavaScript code in all the correct places, and we've added the required HTML `data` attribute to connect our Stimulus controller to our HTML. The last thing to do is to add our Prism CSS into our application. We already have our `prism.css` CSS file in place, we just need to load it. Let's add this to the bottom of our `application.scss` file:

```
@import './prism';
```

This is similar to adding a `<link>` tag into our HTML to load a CSS file. With this modification, we now get colors and other styling, as shown in Figure 14-8, for our `code` blocks.

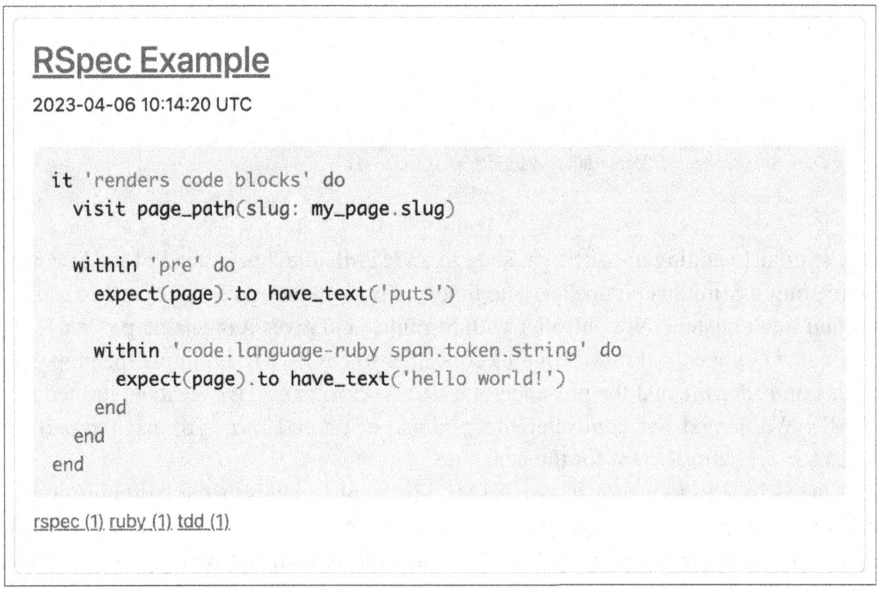

RSpec Example

2023-04-06 10:14:20 UTC

```
it 'renders code blocks' do
  visit page_path(slug: my_page.slug)

  within 'pre' do
    expect(page).to have_text('puts')

    within 'code.language-ruby span.token.string' do
      expect(page).to have_text('hello world!')
    end
  end
end
```

rspec (1), ruby (1), tdd (1)

Figure 14-8 Prism syntax highlighting

Summary

In this chapter, we wrapped up several odds and ends including building a sitemap, adding pagination for our page entries, and adding CSS styling and code syntax highlighting. We also learned a little about Stimulus and Turbo and how to integrate plain old JavaScript into our modern Rails application.

Summary

Bonus: Deploy to Production

15

In this "bonus" chapter, we will deploy our Rails blog application into production. You do not need to read this chapter to complete the book. This chapter is extra, for those who are interested in learning how to deploy a Rails application into production.

We will install and configure Capistrano,[1] a remote server automation and deployment tool, and then command it to perform a repeatable production deployment. On our production server, we will run Debian Linux. We will install and configure Ruby and Phusion Passenger[2] to work with an Apache web server. We will configure Apache to serve our Rails blog application using a `VirtualHost` configuration. We will store our code on GitHub and move things across the Internet securely using SSH.

Why This Non-cloud Approach?

There is presently a push in "the industry" to move away from the cloud-hosting approach and return to deploying to bare metal. The cloud is expensive, and there is needless additional complexity in managing a cloud environment.

The cloud is great for scaling up and down, but if you don't need to scale up and down, then you probably don't need the cloud.

You can discover more information about exiting the cloud here:

https://duckduckgo.com/?q=dhh+exiting+the+cloud

Acquiring a Production Linux Server

In our current age of modern computing, it is very simple and easy to acquire a production Linux server. We can rent a dedicated server from a hosting provider such as Rackspace, DreamHost, or Namecheap. The options are endless.

However you choose to acquire a production Linux server, you will need to have root access to it. This means you will need to be able to log in to the server as the `root` user, or become the root user using `su` or `sudo`, after logging in with your regular unprivileged user account.

---

[1] https://capistranorb.com/

[2] www.phusionpassenger.com/

© The Author(s), under exclusive license to APress Media, LLC, part of Springer Nature 2024
G. Donald, *Hands-on Test-Driven Development*,
https://doi.org/10.1007/978-1-4842-9748-3_15

For the purposes of this book, I will assume that you have acquired a Linux server and that you have root access. I will also assume that you have a domain name that you can use to access your production server. You don't have to have a domain name, but it's a little easier to remember a domain name compared to an IP address.

My production server that I will reference while writing this chapter is an EC2 instance running on Amazon Web Services. I've acquired a t2.micro instance running Debian Linux version 11. I'm using AWS so I can minimize cost. I will delete my server instance after I've written this chapter.

I've acquired a domain name from Namecheap, tdd-book.com, and I've configured it to point to my production server's IP address. None of this will be working anymore by the time you read this book, just so you know.

Getting Production Ready

Before we can deploy our Rails blog application to production, we need to install and configure things on our production server. Our Debian operating system will need to be configured to run Ruby and Phusion Passenger.

Installing Dependencies

Let's install all of our dependencies on our Debian server. We will need to become the root user for all of this to work:

```
sudo su -
```

Then let's install the following packages using the `apt` command:

```
apt update

apt install -y apache2 \
               apache2-dev \
               build-essential \
               git \
               libcurl4-openssl-dev \
               libffi-dev \
               libpq-dev \
               libssl-dev \
               libreadline-dev \
               libyaml-dev \
               postgresql \
               wget \
               zlib1g-dev
```

These are all packages we will get from our Debian operating system repositories. They are not known for being the latest and greatest version; they are instead known for being stable and reliable. We will venture out into more cutting-edge versions of things with our latest version of Ruby and Phusion Passenger however.

Installing Ruby

Continuing as the root user, let's change into our /usr/src directory and download the latest 3.2.2 version of Ruby:

```
cd /usr/src

wget https://cache.ruby-lang.org/pub/ruby/3.2/ruby-3.2.2.tar.gz
```

Next let's extract the archive we downloaded using the tar command:

```
tar xvf ruby-3.2.2.tar.gz
```

Now let's configure, build, and install our new Ruby:

```
cd ruby-3.2.2

./configure

make

make install
```

After Ruby is installed, let's use our new gem command to install the bundler and rack gems:

```
gem install bundler rack
```

Installing Phusion Passenger

Next, let's download the latest 6.0.17 version of Phusion Passenger:

```
cd /usr/src

wget \
https://github.com/phusion/passenger/releases/\
download/release-6.0.17/passenger-6.0.17.tar.gz
```

Be careful with the preceding `wget` command and URL. It's a long URL and is wrapped for use in a shell environment using backslashes. If you copy and paste it into your terminal and it does not work, then you may need to remove the backslashes and paste it in as one long line. If you still have problem, you can instead download the archive file manually from the Phusion Passenger GitHub page:

https://github.com/phusion/passenger/releases

Assuming you downloaded the file without any issues, let's now extract it using the `tar` command:

```
tar xvf passenger-6.0.17.tar.gz
```

Now that we've untarred our Phusion Passenger download, let's install it:

```
cd passenger-6.0.17

bin/passenger-install-apache2-module
```

You will be prompted to answer a question about language support:

```
Which languages are you interested in?
```

Make sure to select `Ruby` using your space bar, and then press `Enter`. Passenger takes a while to build and install. At the end it will prompt us to add a few lines to our Apache configuration file. Let's change into our Apache module directory and create a new file called `passenger.load` and put the following contents in it:

```
cd /etc/apache2/mods-available

# Create a new file called passenger.load with the contents:
LoadModule \
  passenger_module \
  /usr/src/passenger-6.0.17/buildout/apache2/mod_passenger.so
<IfModule mod_passenger.c>
  PassengerRoot /usr/src/passenger-6.0.17
  PassengerDefaultRuby /usr/local/bin/ruby
</IfModule>
```

Then enable our new `passenger.load` file using the `a2enmod` command:

```
a2enmod passenger
```

Next, we need to disable the Apache mpm_event module using the a2dismod command; we're not going to be using it and it's on by default:

```
a2dismod mpm_event
```

We're going to use the Apache mpm_prefork module instead. We need to enable it and some other Apache modules that we will also need for our Rails application:

```
a2enmod auth_digest \
        headers \
        mpm_prefork \
        proxy \
        proxy_http \
        rewrite \
        socache_shmcb \
        ssl
```

Now we can restart our Apache web server and see that we have no errors from our Phusion Passenger install and our module updates:

```
service apache2 restart
```

Finally, let's modify our PATH to include the Passenger bin directory. Let's add the following line to the end of our /etc/bash.bashrc file:

```
export PATH="/usr/src/passenger-6.0.17/bin:$PATH"
```

Configuring PostgreSQL

We installed PostgreSQL earlier, but we still need to configure it. Let's change into our /etc/postgresql/13/main directory and make some additions to our postgresql.conf file:

```
client_min_messages = warning
```

This lets PostgreSQL listen on all network interfaces, and it also sets the minimum level of messages that PostgreSQL will log. We want logging but we don't want to log everything, just warnings and errors. The log levels below "*warning*" are very noisy and not very useful.

Next, let's modify our `pg_hba.conf` file to allow us to connect to PostgreSQL locally. We'll add the following lines near the end of the file:

```
# TYPE  DATABASE  USER  ADDRESS  METHOD
local   all       all            trust
```

This lets us connect to PostgreSQL locally without a password. If you're running a shared server with multiple applications using the same PostgreSQL database instance, then you should instead use the md5 option and set passwords for all your PostgreSQL users.

Now we can restart our PostgreSQL service and see that we have no errors:

```
service postgresql restart
```

Again, as the root user, let's now switch users and create a new PostgreSQL user named admin and give them ownership of a new database:

```
su - postgres

createuser admin

createdb blog -O admin
```

Now that we have a PostgreSQL *admin* user and a *blog* database, let's try them out using the `psql` command:

```
psql -U admin -d blog
```

We should be able to successfully connect to our new blog database as our new admin user and see that we currently have no tables:

```
blog=> \dt
Did not find any relations.
```

PostgreSQL is now configured. Our Rails app will be able to connect to our `blog` database using our `admin` user when we deploy it shortly.

Storing Code on GitHub

You can store your code anywhere you like, but for this chapter, I will assume that you have a GitHub account and that you have stored your code from this book on GitHub. Hopefully, you've been following along and have already done this. If not, read on.

If you don't have a GitHub account, you can create one for free at

https://github.com

Just to be clear, there is no particular reason why I'm using GitHub. It's just a popular place to store code, it's free, and I'm making the assumption that most of my readers will use it or will at least be familiar with it.

If you're using something else, then it will probably just be a matter of different URLs when we configure our deployment.

Installing Capistrano

Capistrano is a Ruby gem, so we can add it to our Rails blog application by modifying our `Gemfile` to add the following in our `development` group:

```
gem "capistrano-rails", "~> 1.6"
gem "capistrano-passenger", "~> 0.2.1"
```

These are the latest versions of those gems at the time of writing. You can probably use newer versions without any significant changes. We're using the `capistrano-rails` gem which will install the `capistrano` gem for us as a dependency. We're also using the `capistrano-passenger` gem which will provide us with some Capistrano Rake tasks to help us more easily work with Phusion Passenger and Apache.

Now let's install these gems into our application by running the `bundle` command.

Configuring Capistrano

Now that we have our Capistrano gems installed, we need to integrate them into our Rails application. We can do this by running the `cap install` command:

```
be cap install
```

This command will add several new files to our Rails application:

```
Capfile
config/deploy.rb
config/deploy/production.rb
config/deploy/staging.rb
```

We can delete or ignore the `staging.rb` file; we're not going to be using it. We will make modifications to the other three files. Let's first modify our `Capfile` file and uncomment the functionality we want to use:

```
require "capistrano/bundler"
require "capistrano/rails/assets"
require "capistrano/rails/migrations"
require "capistrano/passenger"
```

We need bundler support to install our application's Ruby gems on our server. We need Rails asset support to compile our assets. We need Rails migration support to run our database migrations, and we need Passenger support to restart our application after we deploy it.

Next, we need to configure our `config/deploy.rb` file. We'll start by adding the following lines to the top of the file:

```
set :application, 'blog'
set :repo_url, 'git@github.com:gdonald/blog.git'
set :branch, 'main'

append :linked_files, 'config/database.yml',
                      'config/secrets.yml',
                      'config/storage.yml'

append :linked_dirs, 'storage',
                     'log',
                     'tmp/pids',
                     'tmp/cache',
                     'tmp/sockets',
                     'public/system'

set :passenger_restart_with_touch, true
```

There are a number of variables being configured, so let's run through them. First, we set our `application` variable to the name of our application. It's normally used in the name of our application's directory on our server. Next, we define our `repo_url` variable to the URL of our GitHub repository, and we set our `branch` variable to the name of the branch we want to deploy. We're using the `main` branch, but you can use whatever branch you like.

The next two variables, linked_files and linked_dirs, are files and directories that are shared between each deployment we perform. They exist only once on our server and get relinked on each deployment.

The last configuration file we will update is named for the environment we will deploy to, our config/deploy/production.rb file. We need to add the following lines to the top of the file:

```
server 'tdd-book.com', user: 'admin', roles: %w[app db web]
set :deploy_to, '/rails/blog'
set :rails_env, 'production'

set :pty, true
set :ssh_options, {
  forward_agent: true,
  auth_methods: ['publickey'],
  keys: ['~/aws.pem']
}
```

First is our server variable which defines the server we will deploy to. This is a fully qualified domain name, and the username is the user we will use to connect to the server. We're using our default Debian admin user, but you should use the username of your user. The roles are default for our Rails application because our application code and database are both on the same server.

Next, we set our deploy_to variable to the directory where we will deploy. This is a full path on our production server for which our user owns and has write access. Your deploy_to can be different, of course.

Next, we set our rails_env variable to the environment we will deploy to. For our production Rails application, this will be production.

The next two variables are used to configure our SSH connection to our server. We're using Capistrano to issue commands over a pseudo terminal, so we need to set our pty variable to true. After that, we set our ssh_options variable to a hash of options. Inside there, we're telling Capistrano to use the forward_agent option to simplify deploying to our remote server. This will allow a remote SSH agent to securely use our local SSH keys.

Last, we're telling Capistrano with our auth_methods option to use publickey authentication, and then we define the local path to our public key file. This key was automatically added to the authorized_keys file in our ~/.ssh directory when creating the EC2 instance on AWS.

Deploying Our Rails Application

On our production server, we need to create the directory we defined in our deploy_to variable. We can create this directory and change its ownership with the following commands:

```
mkdir -p /rails/blog

chown -R admin:admin /rails
```

Now we can begin to debug our deploy. There are several more steps to perform, but I want to work through each one of them as if we were doing test-driven development. Seeing these errors and fixing them will help us understand what is happening and why.

The command we need to run is

```
cap production deploy
```

The first error we get is

```
01 git@github.com: Permission denied (publickey).
01
01 fatal: Could not read from remote repository.
01
01 Please make sure you have the correct access rights
01 and the repository exists.
```

We're getting this error because we have not yet put a copy of our public key from our production server into our GitHub account. We can do this by navigating to our GitHub account's Settings page and then clicking SSH and GPG keys. We can then click the New SSH key button and paste in the contents of our ~/.ssh/id_rsa.pub file. We can then click the Add SSH key button.

If you find you don't have a ~/.ssh/id_rsa.pub file, you can create one with the following command:

```
ssh-keygen -t rsa
```

This will generate a new key pair and will place the public key contents you need for GitHub in the ~/.ssh/id_rsa.pub file.

Now we can try to deploy again:

```
cap production deploy
```

The next error we get is

```
00:01 deploy:check:linked_files
ERROR linked file /rails/blog/shared/config/database.yml does not
exist on tdd-book.com
```

This error is telling us that we need to create our Rails `database.yml` file on our production server in our /rails/blog/shared/config directory. The contents of this file should match our PostgreSQL user and database names we created earlier. The content of the file should look similar to this:

```
default: &default
  adapter: postgresql
  encoding: unicode
  pool: <%= ENV.fetch("RAILS_MAX_THREADS") { 5 } %>
  port: <%= ENV['DB_PORT'] || 5432 %>

production:
  <<: *default
  database: blog
  username: admin
```

Re-running our deploy command gives us our next error message:

```
00:01 deploy:check:linked_files
ERROR linked file /rails/blog/shared/config/secrets.yml does not
exist on tdd-book.com
```

Rails needs to keep secrets, so it uses a `secrets.yml` file to store a secret key base value that is used to encrypt cookies and other sensitive information. We need to provide this file like we did with our `database.yml` file. The contents of our `secrets.yml` file should look similar to this:

```
production:
  secret_key_base: "make_this_a_long_string_of_random_characters"
```

Make sure and replace the value of `secret_key_base` with a long string of random characters. You can generate a random string of characters with the following command:

```
rake secret
```

Re-running our deploy command gives us our next error message:

```
00:01 deploy:check:linked_files
ERROR linked file /rails/blog/shared/config/storage.yml does not
exist on tdd-book.com
```

Our Rails application uses Active Storage to manage our uploaded images. We need to provide a `storage.yml` file to configure Active Storage for production. The contents of our `storage.yml` file should look similar to this:

```
local:
  service: Disk
  root: <%= Rails.root.join("storage") %>
```

This tells Active Storage to store our uploaded image files in the relative path of `storage` inside our `/rails/blog/shared` directory, which in effect means a full path of `/rails/blog/shared/storage`. Considering that you need to keep this directory backed up, you may not like this, so feel free to change it to a more convenient path for your particular backup strategy.

Re-running our deploy command gives us our next error message:

```
bundle stdout: Your bundle only supports platforms ["arm64-darwin-22"]
but your local platform is x86_64-linux. Add the current platform to
the lockfile with `bundle lock --add-platform x86_64-linux` and try
again.
```

I wrote this book and all the Ruby and Rails code on an arm64 Macbook Pro, but we're trying to deploy to an x86_64 Linux server. Bundler is understandably complaining that we have a platform mismatch in our Gemfile.lock file. We need to add our production platform to our Gemfile.lock file. We can do this by running the command the error message suggests:

```
bundle lock --add-platform x86_64-linux
```

After we run this command, we need to commit the changes and push them up to GitHub, or wherever you're storing your code. We can then re-run our deploy command to get our next error message:

```
ExecJS::RuntimeUnavailable: Could not find a JavaScript runtime. See
\url{https://github.com/rails/execjs} for a list of available runtimes.
```

This error is telling us that we need to install a JavaScript runtime. We need a JavaScript runtime for the Rails asset pipeline to compile our CSS and JavaScript assets. We can remedy this error by installing Node.js.

The version of Node.js available to use from the Debian repositories is too old and does not work with Rails Turbo, so we need to install a newer version from an alternate source. We can install it from *nodesource.com*.[3] To do this, we need to run the following commands:

```
curl -fsSL https://deb.nodesource.com/setup_18.x | bash - &&\
apt-get install -y nodejs
```

This will get us the latest stable version of Node.js. We can then re-run our deploy command to get our next error message:

```
rake stdout: sh: 1: yarn: not found
```

This error message is telling us that we need to install the `yarn` package, a different package manager that we need to assist with compiling our Rails assets. We can do this by running the following commands:

```
npm install yarn -g
```

This command uses `npm`, the node package manager, to install the latest version of `yarn`. The `-g` option tells `npm` to install the `yarn` package globally, so it will be available to all users on our production system, not just the root user performing the install. We can then re-run our deploy command again, and this time we should get a successful deploy with no error messages.

When we now visit our domain name on our production server (mine is at http://tdd-book.com), we do not yet see our Rails app running. We instead see the default Apache web server page. This is because we need to configure our Apache web server's virtual host configuration, to serve our Rails app using Phusion Passenger.

Configuring Our Apache Virtual Host

We currently have the default Apache web server configuration serving up content from the `/var/www/html` directory under a single virtual host entry. The configuration file representing the virtual host is located in the `/etc/apache2/sites-available` directory and is named `000-default.conf`. We need to modify it to serve up content from our `/rails/blog/current/public` directory instead.

Let's update the file to look like this:

```
<VirtualHost *:80>
  ServerAdmin admin@tdd-book.com
  SetEnv RAILS_ENV production
```

---

[3]https://github.com/nodesource/distributions

```
  ServerName tdd-book.com
  ServerAlias www.tdd-book.com
  DocumentRoot /rails/blog/current/public
  <Directory /rails/blog/current/public>
    Require all granted
    Options -MultiViews
  </Directory>
  ErrorLog ${APACHE_LOG_DIR}/error.log
  CustomLog ${APACHE_LOG_DIR}/tdd-book.com.log combined
</VirtualHost>
```

Be sure to update the `Server*` values to match your own domain name and email address.

Notice that we've added the `SetEnv RAILS_ENV` line to tell our Rails app that we're running in a production environment. This is important, because it will tell our Rails app to use our production database configuration in our `database.yml` file, and not look for the default *development* database configuration.

There's also some magic here. Phusion Passenger knows our virtual host is now configured as a Rails app. When we make some future updates and redeploy our Rails app, Capybara can automatically let Passenger know it needs to hot-reload the new version of our code. We will have zero downtime on redeploys.

Using Passenger as an Apache web server module, we automatically get all the decades of effort that have gone into making Apache a stable, secure, and performant web server. We also get the ability to automatically serve up static assets from our `public` directory, which is a "*really nice to have*" feature in not having to configure another web server on another port or adding additional configuration to our virtual host entry just to match incoming requests for them.

After we make these virtual host changes, we need to restart our Apache web server:

```
service apache2 restart
```

Logging In

We can now visit our domain name in our web browser and see our Rails app running, but we cannot yet log in to our admin to add any new page content. We do not currently have a user account in our production database. Let's add one using our Rails console:

```
RAILS_ENV=production bundle exec rails c
```

This will open a Rails console into our production environment connected to our production database. We can now create a new user account using our user Factory:

```
FactoryBot.create(:user,
                   name: 'Greg Donald',
                   email: 'gdonald@gmail.com',
                   password: 'changeme',
                   password_confirmation: 'changeme')
```

Now we can log in to our admin using the email address and password we just created. We can then add some content to our blog.

Summary

In this chapter, we learned how to deploy our Rails app to a production server. We set up a Debian Linux server from scratch, installed all the necessary packages and dependencies, and configured our Apache web server to run Phusion Passenger to serve our Rails app. We also learned how to use Capybara to automatically deploy our Rails app to our production server.

Index

Printed in the United States
by Baker & Taylor Publisher Services